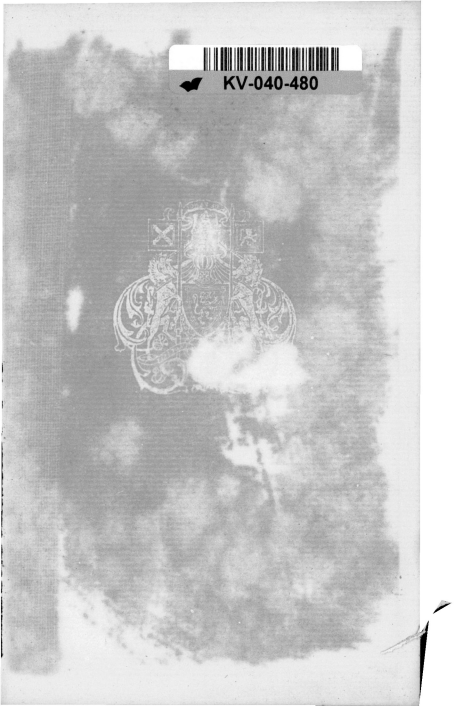

ALLAN
RAMSAY

ALLAN: RAMSAY

BY OLIPHANT : :SMEATON

FAMOUS SCOTS: SERIES

PUBLISHED BY
OLIPHANT ANDERSON
& FERRIER·EDINBVRGH
AND LONDON

The designs and ornaments of this volume are by Mr. Joseph Brown, and the printing from the press of Messrs. Morrison & Gibb, Edinburgh.

PREFACE

SINCE this Volume was in type, I have received some additional information which I feel constrained to lay before my readers.

With reference to the Easy Club, I have been favoured, through the courtesy of the Rev. Dr. A. B. Grosart, with a sight of the complete Minutes of the Club. From them I observe that Ramsay was one of the earliest members admitted, and that his song 'Were I but a Prince or King' was formally presented to the Club after his admission not before, though its rough draft must have been shown to the members prior to that event.

Next, as regards the Editions of *The Gentle Shepherd*, a valued correspondent, Mr. J. W. Scott, Dowanhill, Glasgow, kindly calls my attention to two 'Translations into English' of the Poem which appear to have hitherto escaped notice. These are '*Allan Ramsay's Gentle Shepherd, translated into English by W. Ward, 8vo, 1785.*' Ward, as Mr. Scott states, seems to have been a 'naturalised Englishman' residing at Musselburgh. Five years after Ward's production, appeared another, and in many respects a better Edition, to wit, '*The Gentle Shepherd, a Scotch Pastoral by Allan Ramsay, Attempted in English by Margaret Turner, London, 1790.*' It was dedicated to the Prince of Wales, and its list of Subscribers contains the names of most of the nobility of Scotland. Is this not a reliable gauge of the popularity of the Poem?

EDINBURGH, *March* 1896.

CONTENTS

CHAPTER VII

CHAPTER VIII

CHAPTER IX

CHAPTER X

CHAPTER XI

CHAPTER XII

ALLAN RAMSAY

CHAPTER I

THE FAMILY TREE

'YE'D better let me gang doon wi' the wig, Miss Kirsty,' said Peggy, the 'serving-lass' in the household of Mr. James Ross, writer, of the Castlehill.

'Oh no! I'd as leif take it doon mysel' to Allan Ramsay's, for the sake o' the walk and the bit crack wi' the canty callant,' replied the young lady, a blush crimsoning her fair, rounded cheek.

And Peggy would retire from these periodical but good-humoured passages-at-arms, with a knowing smile on her face, to confide the fact, mayhap,—of course as a profound secret,—to her cronies in the same stair, that Miss Kirsty Ross was 'unco ta'en up wi' that spruce genty wigmaker, Maister Allan Ramsay, doon ayont the Tron Kirk.'

Yea! verily, it was a love drama, but as yet only in the first scene of the first act. The 'Miss Kirsty' of the brief dialogue recorded above—for the authenticity of which there is abundant evidence—was Miss Christian Ross, eldest daughter of Mr. James Ross, a lawyer of some repute in his day, whose practice lay largely in the

Bailie's and Sheriff's Courts, and with minor cases in the Justiciary Court, but not with civil business before the Court of Session, an honour rigorously reserved for the members of that close Corporation—the Writers to His Majesty's Signet.

But though not belonging, in slang phrase, 'to the upper crust' of the legal fraternity, James Ross was a man of some social consideration. Though he appears to have had a strain of the fashionable Pharisee in him, and to have esteemed gentle birth as covering any multitude of sins and peccadilloes, he manifested, throughout his intercourse with Ramsay, certain countervailing virtues that render him dear to the lovers of the poet. He made distinct pretensions to the possession of culture and a love of *belles-lettres*. To the best Edinburgh society of the period he and his had the *entrée*, while his house in Blair's Close, on the southern slope of the Castlehill, was the rendezvous for most of the *literati* of the city, as well as for the *beaux esprits* of the Easy Club, of which he was a member.

His acquaintance with the young wigmaker—whose sign of the 'Mercury,' situate in the High Street, or, as the poet himself writes, 'on Edinburgh's Street the sun-side,' was almost immediately opposite Niddry's Wynd, and at the head of Halkerston's Wynd, and within sixty yards of the Tron Church—had originated in the weekly visits paid by him to Allan's shop for the purpose of getting his wig dressed. While waiting until this important item in an eighteenth-century gentleman's toilet was accomplished, he had enjoyed many a 'crack' with the young craftsman, so shrewd, so witty, so genial, yet withal so industrious. The man of pleas and precepts discovered him of powder and perukes to be as deeply interested and, in good sooth, as deeply versed in the literature of his own land as the lawyer himself. Chance acquaintance gradually ripened, on both sides, into cordial esteem. James Ross invited Ramsay to visit him at his house, and there the young *perruquier* beheld his fate in Christian, or Kirsty, Ross.

If Allan were fascinated by Kirsty's rare beauty and piquant *espièglerie*, by her sweet imperiousness and the subtle charm of her refined femininity, exercised on a nature whose previous experience of the sex had been limited to the bare-legged Amazons of Leadhills or the rosy-cheeked ministering Hebes, whom the high wages of domestic service attracted to town ; she, in turn, was no less captivated by the manly, self-possessed demeanour, and the ingratiating qualities, both social and intellectual, of her father's guest. If he had mingled too little with society for his manners to be tinged with the polish of the *débonnair* gallant, his natural good - breeding and ready tact, united, it must be confessed, to a not inconsiderable spice of vanity, doubtless prevented any lapse into those nervous *gaucheries* wherewith a youth's first appearance in good society is often accompanied.

Allan has drawn with truth and graphic power his own portrait as he appeared at this time—

> ' *Imprimis*—then for tallness I
> Am five feet and four inches high ;
> A black-a-vic'd, snod, dapper fellow,
> Nor lean, nor overlaid wi' tallow ;
> With phiz of a Morocco cut,
> Resembling a late man of wit,
> Auld-gabbet Spec, who was so cunning
> To be a dummie ten years running.

> Then for the fabric of my mind,
> 'Tis more to mirth than grief inclined ;
> I rather choose to laugh at folly
> Than show dislike by melancholy :
> Well judging a sour heavy face
> Is not the truest mark of grace.'

Existing portraits, including the one most valued for its fidelity to the original, that by his son, Allan Ramsay, the artist (Portrait-painter in Ordinary to King George III.), show him to have possessed features that were delicate and sharply chiselled, keen dark eyes, a mobile, sensitive mouth, a complexion dark almost to swarthiness, and a high rounded forehead. To these items may be added those others coming as side-lights, thrown on a man's character and individuality by the passing references of contemporaries. From such sources we learn that his face was one whereon were writ large, contentment with himself and with the world, as well as a certain pawky shrewdness and unaffected *bonhomie*. This expression was largely induced by the twinkling of his beadlike eyes, and the lines of his mouth, which curved upwards at the corners ; almost imperceptibly, it is true, yet sufficiently to flash into his countenance that subtle element of humorous *canniness* which has been accepted by many as the prime attribute of his character. He may probably have had his own feelings in view when he makes his Patie say in *The Gentle Shepherd*—

> ' The bees shall loath the flow'r, and quit the hive,
> The saughs on boggy ground shall cease to thrive,
> Ere scornfu' queans, or loss o' warldly gear,
> Shall *spill* my rest, or ever force a tear.'

His figure was thickset, but had not as yet acquired the squatness of later days. If in the years to come he grew to resemble George Eliot's portrait of Mr. Casson, when the inevitable penalty of sedentariness and good living has to be paid in increasing corpulence, he never lost his tripping gait which in early manhood earned for him the *sobriquet* of 'Denty Allan.' In deportment and dress he was 'easy, trig and neat,' leaning a little to vanity's side in his manners, yet nathless as honourable, sound-hearted, clean-souled a gentleman as any that lounged around Edinburgh Cross of a sunny Saturday afternoon. Such was the youth that presented himself to bonny Kirsty Ross at her father's tea-table.

The acquaintance soon expanded into friendship. Before long, as has been stated, the household observed, not without amusement, that whenever Saturday came round, on which day James Ross' wig was sent down to receive its week's dressing from young Ramsay, Kirsty found she needed a walk, which always seemed to take her past the sign of 'the flying Mercury,' so that she could hand in the wig and call for it as she returned. Ah, artful Miss Kirsty! As the idyll progressed, the interim walk was abandoned, and the fair one found it pleasanter, as she said, to pass the time in conversation with the young *coiffeur* as he combed the paternal wig. The intercourse thus commenced on both sides, more as a frolic than aught else, speedily led to warmer feelings than those of friendship being entertained, and in the spring of 1711 Allan Ramsay asked the daughter of the lawyer to share life's lot with him.

The lovers were, of course, too well aware of the dissimilarity in their social stations to hope for any ready acquiesence in their matrimonial projects by the ambitious Edinburgh lawyer. To win consent, the matter had to

be prudently gone about. The position Ramsay's family
had held in the past reckoned for something, it is true,
in the problem, but the real point at issue was, What
was the social status of the swain at that moment? Ah,
there was the rub! All very well was it for a literary-
minded lawyer to patronise his wigmaker by inviting him
to drink a dish of tea with his family, or to crack a bottle
with him over Jacobite plots or the latest poems of Swift
or Pope; but to give him his daughter in marriage, that
was altogether another question. Mrs. Grundy was
quite as awe-inspiring a dame then as now. James Ross
and his spouse would require to make a careful investi-
gation into the pedigree of the 'mercurial' artist in
crinology—to import a trade term of the present into
the staid transactions of the past—before such an alliance
could be thought of. Many and long were the family
councils held. Every item of his descent, his relatives,
his character, his prospects, was discussed, and this is
what they discovered.

Allan Ramsay was born on the 15th of October 1686,
in the little town of Leadhills, situate in the parish of
Crawfordmuir, in the upper ward of Lanarkshire, and in
the very heart of the bleak, heathy Lowther hills. The
house wherein he saw the light is now 'a broken-down
byre,' according to Dr. John Brown in *Horæ Subsecivæ*.
Standing, as it does, 1400 feet above the level of the sea,
the village is chiefly notable as being the most elevated
inhabited ground in Scotland. The industry of the district, then as now, was almost entirely devoted to lead-
mining. The superior of the parish was the Earl of
Hopetoun, and on his behoof the mines were wrought.
The male population, with but few exceptions, were in

his lordship's service. A more desolate and dreary spot could scarcely be conceived. The rugged ranges, destitute of wood, were scarred by the traces of former workings, and intersected, moreover, by narrow rocky ravines, down which brawled foaming mountain burns. Perched like an eyrie on some steep cliff, the view from the vicinity of the town is magnificent, ranging over fair Clydesdale, and the lands formerly owned by the Earls of Crawford, 'the Lindsays, light and gay,' whose ancient castle stands on Clydeside.

In the days of the Stuarts gold used to be found in considerable quantities in the locality, from which was struck the gold issue bearing the head of James V., wearing a bonnet; hence the old term for it—a 'bonnet-piece.'

The inhabitants of the town and district of Leadhills had imbibed in Ramsay's days something of the stern, forbidding character of the scenery. The ruggedness of their surroundings had evidently sunk deep into their temperament,—and ofttimes the teaching of nature in situations like this is of the most lasting kind. So it was with them. They were a community apart : gloomily, almost fanatically, religious; believing in miracles, visions, and in the direct interposition of Providence,—in a word, carrying to the extreme of bigotry all the grand attributes of Scottish Presbyterianism and Covenanting sublimity of motive. They married and gave in marriage among themselves, looking the while rather askance at strangers as 'orra bodies' from the big world without, who, because they *were* strangers, ran a strong chance of being no better than they should be !

To this 'out-of-the-way' corner of the planet there was sent, towards the close of the year 1684, as manager of Lord Hopetoun's mines, a gay, happy-hearted, resourceful young Scotsman, by name Robert Ramsay. The poet, when detailing his pedigree to the father of his *inamorata*, had boasted that he was descended, on the paternal side, from the Ramsays of Dalhousie (afterwards Earls of that Ilk). Such was literally the case. Ramsay of Dalhousie had a younger brother, who, from the estate he held—a small parcel of the ancestral acres—bore a name, or rather an *agnomen*, yet to be historic in song, 'The Laird of Cockpen.' Whether in this case, like his descendant of ballad fame, the said laird was 'proud and great'; whether his mind was 'ta'en up wi' things o' the State,' history doth not record. Only on one point is it explicit, that, like his successor, he married a wife, from which union resulted Captain John Ramsay, whose only claim to remembrance is that he in turn married Janet Douglas, daughter of Douglas of Muthil, and thus brought the poet into kin-ship with yet another distinguished Scottish family. To the captain and his spouse a son was born, who devoted himself to legal pursuits, was a writer in Edinburgh, and acted as legal agent for the Earl of Hopetoun. Through his interest with the earl, Robert Ramsay, his eldest son, was appointed manager of the lead mines in the Lowther hills, and set out to assume his new duties towards the close of the year 1684.

From this pedigree, therefore, the fact is clear of the poet's right to address William Ramsay, Earl of Dal-housie, in terms imitated from Horace's famous Ode to Maecenas—

> 'Dalhousie, of an auld descent,
>   My chief, my stoup, my ornament.'

But to our narrative. Apparently the young mine-manager found the lines of his life by no means cast in pleasant places amid the rough semi-savage community of Leadhills in those days. He felt himself a stranger in a strange land. To better his lot, though he was still very young, he determined to marry. The only family with which he could hold intercourse on terms of equality, was that of William Bower, an English mineralogist who had been brought from Derbyshire, to instruct the Scottish miners more fully in the best methods then known for extracting the metal from the refractory matrix. But to Robert Ramsay the chief attraction in the family was the eldest daughter of his colleague, Alice Bower, a vivacious, high - spirited girl, with a sufficient modicum, we are told, of the Derbyshire breeziness of nature to render her invincibly fascinating to the youth. Alone of all those around she reminded him of the fair dames and damsels of Edinburgh. Therefore he wooed and won her. Their marriage took place early in January 1686. In the October of the same year the future poet was born.

But, alas! happiness was not long to be the portion of the wedded pair. At the early age of twenty-four Robert Ramsay died, leaving his widow, as regards this world's gear, but indifferently provided for, and, moreover, burdened with an infant scarce twelve months old.

Probably the outlook for the future was so dark that the young widow shrank from facing it. Be this as it may, we learn that three months after Robert Ramsay was laid in his grave she married David Crichton, finding a home for herself and a stepfather for the youthful Allan at one and the same time. Crichton was a small peasant-proprietor, or bonnet-laird, of the district. Though not endowed with much wealth, he seems to have been in fairly comfortable circumstances, realising his step-son's ideal in after-life, which he put into the mouth of his Patie—

> ' He that hath just enough can soundly sleep ;
> The o'ercome only fashes fouk to keep.'

Much has been written regarding the supposed un-happiness of Ramsay's boyhood in the household of his step-parent. For such a conclusion there is not a tittle of evidence. Every recorded fact of their mutual re-lations points the other way. David Crichton was evidently a man of high moral principle and strength of character. Not by a hairbreadth did he vary the treatment meted out to Allan from that accorded to his own children by the widow of Robert Ramsay. To the future poet he gave, as the latter more than once testified, as good an education as the parish school afforded. That it embraced something more than the 'three R's,' we have Ramsay's own testimony, direct and indirect— direct in the admission that he had learned there to read Horace 'faintly in the original'; indirect in the number and propriety of the classical allusions in his works. He lived before the era of quotation books and dictionaries of phrase and fable,—the hourly godsend of the penny-a-liner ; but the felicity of his references is unquestion-able, and shows an acquaintance with Latin and English literature both wide and intimate. At anyrate, his scholastic training was sufficiently catholic to imbue his mind with a reverence for the masterpieces in both languages, and to enable him to consort in after years, on terms of perfect literary equality, with the lawyers and the *beaux esprits* of witty Edinburgh, such as Dr. Pitcairn, Dr. Webster, and Lord Elibank.

Until his migration to the Scottish capital, at the age of fifteen, Ramsay was employed, during his spare hours, in assisting his stepfather in the work of the farm. The intimate acquaintance he displays in his pastoral with the life and lot of the peasant-farmer, was the result of his early years of rural labour among the Lowther hills. That they were years of hardship, and a struggle at hand-grips with poverty, goes without the saying. The land around the Lowthers was not of such a quality as to render the bonnet-laird's exchequer a full one. As a shepherd, therefore, young Ramsay had to earn hardly the bread he ate at his stepfather's table. The references to his vocation are numerous in his poems. In his Epistle to his friend William Starrat, teacher of mathematics at Straban in Ireland, he adverts to his early life—

> 'When speeling up the hill, the dog-days' heat
> Gars a young thirsty shepherd pant and sweat;
> I own 'tis cauld encouragement to sing,
> When round ane's lugs the blattran hailstanes ring;
> But feckfu' fouk can front the bauldest wind,
> And slunk through muirs, an' never fash their mind.
> Aft hae I wade through glens wi' chorking feet,
> When neither plaid nor kilt could fend the weet;
> Yet blythly wad I bang out o'er the brae,
> And stend o'er burns as light as ony rae,
> Hoping the morn might prove a better day.'

The boy, meantime, must have been photographing on the retentive negatives of his mind the varied scenes of rural life, the labours incidental to the alternating seasons, which he was to employ with effect so rare in his inimitable pastoral. During the winter months, when the snow lay deep on hill and glen, over scaur and cleugh among the lonely Lowthers, when the flocks were 'faulded' and the 'kye' housed in the warm byres, when the furious blasts, storming at window and door, and the deadly nipping frost, rendered labour outside impracticable, doubtless in David Crichton's household, as elsewhere over broad Scotland, the custom prevailed of sitting within the *lum-cheek* of the cavernous fireplaces, or around the *ingle-neuk*, and reciting those ancient ballads of the land's elder life, that had been handed down from True Thomas and the border minstrels; or narrating those tales of moving accidents by flood or field, of grim gramarye, and of the mysterious sights and sounds of other days, whose memory floated down the stream of popular tradition from age to age. In days when books were so costly as to be little more than the luxury of the rich, the art of the fireside rhapsodist was held in a repute scarcely less high, than in that epoch which may justly be styled the period of Grecian romance—the days of 'the blind old man of Scio's rocky isle.' At that spring there is abundant evidence that young Allan Ramsay had drunk deep.

To another well, also, of genuine inspiration he must by this time have repaired—that of our native Scottish literature. Though some years had yet to elapse before he could read Hamilton of Gilbertfield's poem, the 'Dying Words of Bonnie Heck,' which he afterwards praised as stimulating him into emulation, there is little doubt he had already caught some faint echoes of that glorious period in Scottish literature, which may be said to have lasted from the return of the poet-king (James I.) in 1424, from his captivity in England, to the death of

Drummond of Hawthornden in 1649. Without taking account of Barbour's *Bruce* and Blind Harry's *Wallace*, which partake more of the character of rhyming chronicles than poems,—though relieved here and there by passages of genuine poetic fire, such as the familiar one in the former, beginning—

> ' Ah ! fredome is a nobill thynge,
> Fredome maks men to haiff liking,'

—the literary firmament that is starred at the period in question with such names as King James I., Robert Henryson, William Dunbar, Walter Kennedy, Gavin Douglas, Sir David Lyndsay, Alexander Montgomery, William Alexander (Earl of Stirling), Sir Robert Ayton, Robert Sempill, and Drummond of Hawthornden, need not fear comparison with the contemporary poetry of the sister land. The greatest name in the list, that of William Dunbar, was undoubtedly the leading singer of his age in the British Isles, but inacquaintance with his works has prevented his genius obtaining that recognition it deserves. Sir Walter Scott considered Dunbar in most qualities the peer, in some the superior, of Chaucer, and his opinion will be endorsed by all those who are able to read Dunbar with enjoyment. Though Spenser's genius may have had a richer efflorescence than Dunbar's, if the mass of their work be critically weighed, quality by quality, the balance, when struck, would rest remarkably evenly between them. Drummond of Hawthornden is perhaps the most richly-gifted writer in early Scottish literature, as an all-round man of letters. But as a poet the palm must ever remain with Dunbar.

The study of the breaks which occur in the poetic succession of any literature is always interesting. In

English literature such gaps recur, though not with any definite regularity—for example, after the death of Chaucer and Gower, when the prosaic numbers of Occleve and Lydgate were the sole representatives of England's imaginative pre-eminence; and the pen-ultimate and ultimate decades of last century, when Hayley was regarded as their acknowledged master by the younger school of poets. In Scotland, it is to be noted, as Sir George Douglas points out in his standard work, *Minor Scottish Poets*, that from 1617, the date of the publication of Drummond's *Forth Feasting*, until 1721, when Ramsay's first volume saw the light, no singer even of mediocre power appeared in Scotland.

There were editions of many of the poems of James I., Dunbar, Stirling, Drummond, and Sempill, which Ramsay may have seen. But he was more likely to have gained the knowledge we know he possessed of the early literature of his country from the recitals by fireside *raconteurs*, and from the printed sheets, or *broadsides*, hawked about the rural districts of Scotland during the closing decades of the seventeenth and the initial ones of the eighteenth centuries. From specimens of these which I have seen, it is evident that Henryson's *Robene and Makyn*, Dunbar's *Merle and the Nightingale* and the *Thistle and the Rose*, with several of Drummond's and Stirling's poems, were circulated in this way, thus becom-ing familiarly known in rural districts where the volumes of these authors never could have penetrated. On these *broadsides*, then, it must have been that the dormant poetical gifts of the youthful Ramsay were fed, and in after years he showed his liking for this form of publication by issuing his own earlier poems in the same way.

CHAPTER II

As much, perhaps, to obtain release from employment so laborious as that on the farm, as from a desire to be independent, young Ramsay consented to his stepfather's proposal that he should be apprenticed to a wigmaker in Edinburgh.

It has been urged, in proof of Crichton's harshness to his stepson, that Ramsay, after he left Leadhills in 1700, never seems to have had any further intercourse with them. Not so much as a chance reference in a letter reveals that he ever had any future dealings with the Crichton family. But this is not to be wondered at. The fact of the death of his mother in 1700 does not wholly explain the matter, I admit. But we need only recall the exclusive character previously attributed to the people of Leadhills, their antipathy to any intrusion upon them by strangers of any kind, to understand the case. They were a type of Scottish Essenes, a close community, akin to the fisher-communities of Newhaven and Fisherrow, with their distinctive customs, traditions, and prejudices. For a gay young Edinburgh spark such as Ramsay, fond of fine clothes, with a strong spice of vanity and egotism in his nature, to sojourn

23

amongst the *dour*, stolid, phlegmatic miners, would have
been to foster the development of asperities on both
sides, calculated to break off all further intercourse.   Met
they may have, and parted on the terms we surmise,
but of such meeting no hint was ever dropped, and a
veil of separation drops between the household at
Crawfordmuir and the young Jacob who thus was sent
forth, from the shadow of what was to him the paternal
roof, to war with the world at his own charges.   That
David Crichton had done his duty nobly by the lad
was evident; but other children were shooting up to
youth's estate, and when the elder bird was full fledged,
it must e'en take its flight from the parent nest to make
room for others.

There is another view of the case not so creditable
to the future poet, but still within the range of possi-
bility—that the scion of the house of Ramsay, whose
anxiety to let the world know he was of gentle lineage
was so chronic, may have felt himself a cut above the
children of the bonnet-lairdie.   Ramsay's nature was
not one wherein the finer sympathies and delicate regard
for the feelings of others were mortised into a sturdy
independence and a desire to carve his fortunes out of
the block of favouring opportunity.   From start to finish
of his career a subtle egoism, born of his lonely situation in life and fostered by his inordinate vanity, was
his distinguishing trait.   Generous acts he did, benevolent
and kindly on numerous occasions he undoubtedly was,
but his charity was not altruism.   He was not the man
to deny himself for the good of others.

Henceforth Edinburgh was to be Ramsay's life's
home.   He was enrolled as an apprentice early in

January 1701. Although, as an apprentice, he was
obliged to undertake duties distinctly domestic and
menial,—for, in those days of strict social and ecclesiastical discipline, a master was expected to discharge
towards those indentured to him much that appertains
solely to the province of the parent,—still, there would
be many spare hours wherein he would be free to devote
himself to such pursuits as his taste led him.

What induced him to select wig-making as his life's
métier is unknown. Perhaps his stepfather may have
had some friend in that line of business who for 'auld
lang syne' was willing to take the boy and teach him
his trade. There is, of course, the other side of the
question to be taken into account, that the work did
not demand much bodily strength for its successful
prosecution, and that it was cleanly, neat, and artistic.
The recent development of the art of the *coiffeur* in
France, in consequence of the attempts of Louis XIV.
to conceal his natural defects of diminutive stature and
a phenomenally small head,—defects impairing the effect
of that majestic mien which the pupil of Mazarin so
persistently cultivated,—had spread into England, and
thence into Scotland. The enormous periwigs rendered
fashionable by *Le Grand Monarque* admitted of a variety
of artistic treatment. The heyday of wig-making may
therefore be said to have extended over at least the
greater part of Ramsay's career in this branch of trade,
and in his day the poet was reckoned the most ingenious
of Edinburgh *perruquiers*.

Another consideration probably influenced him in his
choice to proceed to Edinburgh. The change to lighter
labour would enable him to filch from hours allocated

to sleep precious moments for private reading, which the arduous nature of his employment at Crawfordmuir had prevented. Besides, he was in a 'city of books'— books only waiting to be utilised. That he did take advantage of his opportunities during his apprenticeship, and that it was at this period that the poetic instinct in him took fire, on coming in contact with the electric genius of Shakespeare, Spenser, Milton, and other master-minds of English literature, is a fact to which he refers more than once in his poems.

From 1701–7,—in other words, from his fifteenth to his twenty-first year,—while he was serving his apprentice-ship, there is a gap in the continuity of the records we have of the poet; a *lacuna* all the more regrettable as these were the true germing years of his genius. Of the name of his trade-master, of the spot where the shop of the latter was situated, of his friends at that time, of his pursuits, his amusements, his studies, we know little, save what can be gathered from chance references in after-life. That they were busy years as regards his trade is certain from the success he achieved in it; and that Ramsay was neither a lazy, thriftless, shiftless, or vicious apprentice his after career effectually proves. That they were happy years, if busy, may, I think, be accepted as tolerably certain, for the native gaiety and hilarity of his temperament underwent no abatement. Whether or not his fashionable Edinburgh relatives took any notice of him, whether he was a guest at his grandfather, the lawyer's house, or whether the latter and his family, hidebound by Edinburgh social restrictions, found it necessary to ignore a Ramsay who soiled his fingers with trade, is unknown. Probably not, for it is matter of tradition that it was the fact of his family connections which weighed with Writer Ross in consenting to the union of his daughter with a tradesman.

In the spring of 1707 Allan Ramsay received back his indentures, signed and sealed, with the intimation from the ancient and honourable ' Incorporation of Wig-makers' that he was free of the craft. He appears almost immediately thereafter to have commenced business on his own account in the Grassmarket, being admitted at the same time, in virtue of being a craftsman of the town, a burgess of the City of Edinburgh. Though no trace can be found that the wigmakers ranked amongst the forty-two incorporated Societies or Guilds of the city (for their name does not appear), that they must have enjoyed the same privileges as the other trades, is evident from the fact of Ramsay being enrolled as a burgess, the moment he had completed his apprentice-ship.

CHAPTER III

AN important stage in Allan Ramsay's life's journey
had now been reached. He was of age, he was a burgess of the town, he was a member, or free, of one of
the most influential of the Crafts, or Guilds, in the
capital, but, greatest step of all, he had started in business
for himself, and had flung himself, with a sort of fierce
determination to succeed, into that hand-to-hand fight
with fortune for the sustenance of life, from which each
of us emerges either made or marred.

At a time when all the youthful Ramsay's faculties
were beginning to be strung to their utmost tension of
achievement, strange would it have been if that of observation were not as eagerly exercised.

Scotland in general, and Edinburgh in particular, were
at this period in the throes of a new political birth. The
epoch of transition commenced in 1707, and ended only
when the dangers of the repeated rebellions of 1715
and 1745 showed the supercilious statesmen by the
Thames—the Harleys, the Walpoles, the Pelhams—that
conciliation, not intimidation, was the card to play in
binding Scotland to her greater neighbour. A patriotism
that had burned clear and unwavering from the days of

Wallace and Bruce to those of the exiled and discredited Stuarts, was not to be crushed out by a band of political wirepullers, by whom State peculation was reduced to an art and parliamentary corruption to a science.

Although the ultimate effects of the Union between England and Scotland were in the highest degree beneficial upon the arts, the commerce, and the literature of the latter, the proximate results were disastrous in the extreme ; yet the step was imperative. So strained had become the relations between the two countries, consequent on the jealousy of English merchants and English politicians, that only two alternatives were possible—war, or the corporate union of the whole island. Yet in Scotland the very mention of Union was sufficient to drive the people into a paroxysm of rage. The religious animosity between the two countries was as important a factor in producing this feeling as any other.

English churchmen boasted that with any such Union would come the restoration of Episcopacy north of the Tweed, and the abolition of the Church of Scotland. The latter retaliated by pushing an Act of Security through the Scottish Legislature, which demanded an oath to support the Presbyterian Church in its integrity from every sovereign on his accession. The Scottish Whigs and the Scottish Jacobites, despite political differences wide as the poles, joined hands in resistance to what they considered the funeral obsequies of Scottish nationality. For a time the horizon looked so lowering that preparations actually were begun in Scotland to accumulate munitions of war.

But the genius, the patience, and withal the firmness, of Lord Somers, the great Whig Richelieu of his time,

gradually overcame all difficulties, though he was reduced
to wholesale bribery of the Scottish peers to effect his
end. As Green puts it : 'The Scotch proposals of a
federative rather than a legislative Union were set aside
by his firmness : the commercial jealousies of the English
traders were put by ; and the Act of Union, as finally
passed in 1707, provided that the two Kingdoms should be
united into one under the name of Great Britain, and that
the succession to the crown of this United Kingdom
should be ruled by the provisions of the English Act of
Settlement. The Scotch Church and the Scotch Law
were left untouched, but all rights of trade were thrown
open, and a uniform system of coinage adopted.'

Of all the negotiations for the consummation of the
Union, Ramsay, doubtless, was an interested spectator.
Patriotic to his heart's core, and sympathising as a
Jacobite with the chivalrous feeling of his nation for
the dynasty they had given to England, and which, after
only eighty-six years of alternate loyalty and revolt, the
Southrons had driven into exile, the keenly observant lad
would follow every detail in the closing chapter of Scotland's history as an independent nation, with a pathetic
and sorrowful interest. Undoubtedly, while yet an
apprentice, with a few months of his time unexpired, he
must have watched the last observance of that ancient
and picturesque spectacle, annually recurring, but now
to be abolished for ever—the 'Riding of the Parliament,'
or the procession of members to the opening of the
sittings in the old Parliament House. Perhaps he may
even have secretly gained admission to overhear the
fiery debates on the Union in that ultimate session of
the Scottish legislature. Certainly he must have been one

of the thousands of spectators who day by day thronged the purlieus of the hall where the national assembly met. Of the rage, brooding and deep, or loud and outspoken, according to temperament, which prevailed amongst the Edinburgh people at the mere idea of Union with the hated 'Southrons,' he must have been a witness. Nay, he may have been an onlooker, if not a participant, in that riot which occurred after all was over,—after Lord-Chancellor Seafield had uttered his brutal *mot*, 'There is the end o' an auld sang,' which gathered up for him the gall of a nation's execration for a century to come ; and after the Commissioners of both nations had retired to sign the Treaty of Union. Not, however, to any of the halls of Court did they retire, but to a dingy cellar (still existing) of a house, 177 High Street, opposite the Tron Church—being nearly torn limb from limb in getting there. Then the mob, suddenly realising that now or never they must

'Awake, arise, or be for ever fallen,'

besieged the cellar, intending to execute Jeddart justice or Lynch law on those they esteemed traitors to their country. Fortunately there was another means of egress ; the party hastily took flight to an arbour in the garden of Moray House, where the remaining signatures were appended, and whence all the Commissioners fled post-haste to England, bearing with them the signed copy of the Treaty.

That stirring time, so pregnant with mighty issues, a time when the weal or the woe of the future British Empire trembled in the balance,—for what of achievement could England alone have accomplished, with

Scotland as a hostile neighbour dogging her heels ?—must of itself have been an education to young Ramsay. It both confirmed his patriotism and widened his political outlook.

Yet when the play was over, the curtain rung down, and the lights gone out, the lapse of time must to him, as to other observers of the period, have driven home with stunning force the conviction that the Union spelled ruin for Scotland as a nation and Edinburgh as a city. For five decades to come a listless apathy, born of despair, strangled Scottish enterprise in its birth. The immediate effect of the Union was a serious diminution in the national trade and commerce. The jealousy of English merchants, as it had frustrated the Darien Scheme in the previous century, now closed every possible avenue of commercial activity for the renumerative utilisation of Scottish capital. 'We are dying by inches,' wrote James, Earl of Bute, to a friend. And the signs of the times did not seem to belie the assertion.

In Edinburgh, also, the change was severely felt. The removal of the Court to London, a hundred and four years before, had drawn a large number of the Scottish nobility to the vortex of fashion. The money they were wont to spend during their stay in Edinburgh, while the Court *season* lasted, was diverted into another channel. The town houses which they had been forced to maintain in the Scottish metropolis, were in many cases relinquished, and the place that so long had known them knew them no more. At that time Scottish merchants and shopkeepers had suffered severely, yet they had the satisfaction of knowing that the seat of Scottish government remained north of the Tweed.

But now a change even more radical was inaugurated. The national Parliament, whose sittings had always necessitated the attendance of a considerable proportion of the nobility and gentry of the country, during a certain part of the year, was merged in that of the larger country. Those of the purely Scottish peerage, whom choice or political duties had retained in Scotland, now found no need to maintain their costly Edinburgh establishments. Many a noble ancestral home, that for three or four hundred years had sheltered the household and retainers of families, whose deeds were interwoven with the historic records of Scotland's most glorious epochs, was now advertised for sale. An exodus to London on a vast scale set in, and the capital of Scotland ere long settled down, in the apathy of despair, to play the *rôle* of a provincial centre. Henceforward her 'paper lords,' otherwise Judges of the Court of Session, were to represent her titled magnates.

The bitterness of spirit which such a course of action as this migration inspired in the minds of the residents of the Scottish capital, Ramsay, as a young journeyman, or as a master craftsman who had only newly commenced business for himself, would fervently reciprocate. In two places at least in his works he pathetically, yet vigorously, protests against the cream of Scottish youth being sent away out of the country.

In one of the most suggestively beautiful of his minor pastorals, *Betty and Kate*, he thus writes—

> ' Far, far, o'er far frae Spey an' Clyde,
>   Stands that great town o' Lud,
> To whilk our best lads rin an' ride,
>   That's like to put us wud [mad];

> For sindle times they e'er come back
>   Wha anes are heftit there ;
> Sure, Bess, thae hills are nae sae black,
>   Nor yet thir [these] howms sae bare.'

And in *The Gentle Shepherd*, after the discovery has been
made of Patie's noble birth, his fellow - herd, Roger,
remarks—

> ' Is not our master an' yoursell to stay
>   Amang us here? or, are ye gawn away
>   To London Court, or ither far aff parts,
>   To leave your ain poor us wi' broken hearts?'

The five intercalary years between Ramsay's commencing in business on his own account and his
marriage, were those which may properly be designated
his intellectual seedtime. That he was exercised over
any of the deeper and more complex problems of life,
death and futurity; that he was hagridden by doubt, or
appalled by the vision of man's motelike finitude when
viewed against the deep background of infinity and
eternity, we have no reason to suppose. Never at any
epoch of his life a 'thinker,' in the true sense of the
word, he was inclined, with the genial insouciant Hedon-
ism always characteristic of him, to slip contentedly into
the Pantheism of Pope, to regard humanity and the world
without as

> —— ' but parts of a stupendous whole
>   Whose body nature is, and God the soul,

—the superficial, ethical principle permeating which is
summed up in the dictum, *Whatever is, is right*. Though
he had no sympathy with the Puritanic austerity of Presbyterianism, albeit a regular attendant on the ministra-
tions of Dr. Webster of the Tolbooth Church, one of the
sections whereinto the magnificent cathedral of St. Giles

was of old divided, he was tinctured neither with French scepticism nor with the fashionable doubts which the earlier deistical writers of the century, Lord Herbert of Cherbury, Shaftesbury, Toland, and Blount, were sowing broadcast over Great Britain. In his *Gentle Shepherd* he makes Jenny, when Glaud, her father, had remarked, with respect to the prevailing disregard of religion and morality among the youth of the better classes,

> —— ' I've heard mysell
> Some o' them laugh at doomsday, sin, and hell,'

make the following reply, which savours strongly of the slippered orthodoxy of *The Essay on Man*—

> ' Watch o'er us, father ! hech, that's very odd ;
> Sure, him that doubts a doomsday, doubts a God.'

But though he appears to have given a wide berth to the ponderous theology, the narrow ethics, and the hair-splitting metaphysics of the time, his whole nature seems to have been stirred and awakened more deeply than ever by his study of the elder poets in English literature. Not that their music tended to make him discontented with his lot, or unhinged the lid of his resolution to become a thoroughly efficient man of business. Ramsay, unlike many of his brethren of the lyre, was of an eminently practical temperament. Rumour says that in earlier boyhood he cherished a desire of becoming an artist. But his stepfather not possessing the means to furnish him with the necessary training, he wisely sloughed all such unreasonable dreams, and aimed at independence through wig-making.

Wisdom as commendable was displayed now. Though his studies must have kindled poetic emulation in him ;

though the vague unexpressed longings of a richly-gifted nature were doubtless daily present with him, no thought ever seems to have entered his mind of relinquishing trade for poetry. On his ambition, also, he kept a steady curb, determining to publish nothing but what his more matured judgment would approve. Not to him in after years would the regret come that he had cursed his fame by immaturity.

From 1707 until 1711, during the dreary depression of the time immediately succeeding the Union, when Scotsmen preferred apathy to action, Ramsay sought surcease from his pangs of wounded patriotism by plunging into studies of various kinds, but principally of English poetry. In a letter, hitherto unpublished, addressed to his friend Andrew Gibb, who appears to have resided at or near West Linton, he remarks: ' I have rowth of good reading to wile my heart from grieving o'er what cannot be mended now,—the sale o' our unhappy country to the Southron alliance by a wheen traitors, who thought more o' Lord Somers' gold than Scotland's rights. In Willie Shakspeare's melodious numbers I forget the dark days for trade, and in auld Chaucer's Tales, and Spenser's ' Queen,' in John Milton's majestic flow, in Giles and Phineas Fletcher, in rare Ben and our ain Drummond, I tine the sorrows o' the day in the glories o' the days that are past.'

That we may accept Ramsay's account of the studies of Patie, the Gentle Shepherd, as a type of his own is warranted by something more than tradition. The internal evidence of his works throws a strong colour of probability over the theory. When Sir William Worthy, who as a Royalist had been compelled to flee into exile during the times of the Commonwealth, inquires what were the books his son, whom he had committed to the care of Symon, his shepherd, to be reared as his own child, was in the habit of reading, the honest old servant replies—

> ' When'er he drives our sheep to Edinburgh port,
> He buys some books o' hist'ry, sangs, or sport;
> Nor does he want o' them a rowth at will,
> And carries aye a poochfu' to the hill.
> Aboot ane Shakspeare—an' a famous Ben,
> He aften speaks, an' ca's them best o' men.
> How sweetly Hawthornden an' Stirling sing,
> An' ane ca'd Cowley, loyal to his king,
> He kens fu' weel, an' gars their verses ring.
> I sometimes thought he made owre great a phrase
> About fine poems, histories, and plays.
> When I reproved him ance, a book he brings,
> "Wi' this," quoth he, "on braes I crack wi' kings."'

By the side-light thrown on Ramsay's life from this passage we gain some idea of his own studies during those years of germination. To the poets more exclusively Scottish, whether writing in the current literary medium of the day or in the vernacular of the country; to Robert Sempill's *Life and Death of the Piper of Kilbarchan*; to William Cleland's *Highland Host*—in addition to Drummond and the Earl of Stirling, mentioned in the passage quoted above; to William Hamilton of Gilbertfield's verses, *The Dying Words of Bonnie Heck*, and to others of less note, he seems to have devoted keen and enthusiastic attention. Lieutenant Hamilton it was (as Ramsay admits in the poetical correspondence maintained between them) who first awakened within him the desire to write in the dialect of his country—

> ' When I begoud first to cun verse,
> And could your "Ardry Whins" rehearse,

Where Bonny Heck ran fast and fierce,
          It warm'd my breast;
  Then emulation did me pierce,
          Whilk since ne'er ceast.'

There was, however, another influence at work, quite
as potent, stimulating his poetic fancy.   Amid the
beauties of the 'Queen of Cities' he lived, and the
charms of his surroundings sank deep into his impres-
sionable nature.   In whatever direction he looked, from
the ridgy heights of the Castlehill, a glorious natural
picture met his eye.   If to the north, his gaze caught
the gleam of the silvery estuary of the Forth, with fertile
reaches of green pasture-land intervening, and the little
villages of Picardy, Broughton, and Canonmills peeping
out from embosoming foliage, while beyond the silver
streak, beautified by the azure enchantment of distance,
glowed in the sunshine the heath-clad Lomonds and the
yellow wealth of the fields of Fife.   Did the youthful
poet turn eastward, from yonder favourite lounge of his
on Arthur Seat, the mouth of the noble Firth, dotted
with sail, was full in view, with the shadowy outlines of
the May Island, peeping out like a spirit from the depth
of distance, and nearer, the conical elevation of North
Berwick Law and the black-topped precipitous mass of
the Bass; while seemingly lying, in comparison, almost
at his feet, was the magnificent semicircular sweep of
Aberlady Bay, with its shore-fringe of whitewashed
villages gleaming like a string of glittering pearls, behind
which stretched the fertile carse of East Lothian, rolling
in gently undulating uplands back to the green Lammer-
moors.   Or if he gazed southward, did his eye not catch
the fair expanse of Midlothian, as richly cultivated as it

was richly wooded, extending before him like a match-less picture, dotted with homesteads, hamlets, and villages, past Dalkeith—'which all the virtues love,' past Lasswade, past Roslin's castled rock, past Dryden's groves of oak, past caverned Hawthornden, until earth and sky seemed to meet in the misty horizon line of the Moorfoots? And westward, was not the eye guided by the grassy grandeur of the Pentland Range, until beauty was merged in indefiniteness across the wide strath lying like a painted scroll from Edinburgh to Linlithgow?

Fairer scene never nurtured poet in 'the fine frenzy of his art'; and in long excursions during his spare hours, amidst the silent glens and frowning *cleughs* of the Pentlands, amidst the romantic scenery clothing the banks of both the Esks, by Almond's gentle flow, and by the wimpling waters of the Water of Leith, our Caledonian Theocritus fed his germing genius on food that was destined to render him at once the greatest and the most breezily objective of British pastoral poets.

From 1707 to 1711 thus did Allan Ramsay 'live and learn,'—a youth whose nature, fired by the memories of Scotland's greatness in years gone by, already longed to add something of value to the cairn of his country's literature. Such, too, were the facts of which, at his request, the worthy lawyer, Mr. James Ross, was placed in possession when he was called on to decide whether his friend, the 'poetically-minded wigmaker,' should be regarded as a *persona grata* from the point of view of a prospective son-in-law. That the 'pedigree' of the young aspirant was accepted as satisfactory may be regarded as certain from the fact that the marriage of Allan Ramsay and Christian Ross was celebrated during

the New Year festivities of 1712. A woman, at once of
considerable personal attractions, sound common sense
and practical knowledge of the world, a capital house-
wife withal, and though not devoid of a certain modicum
of literary appreciation, by no means a blue-stocking,
such, in brief, was the lady who for thirty years was to be
the faithful partner of Ramsay's fortunes, rejoicing with
him in success, sympathising with him in reverse—one
who merited to the full the glowing lines wherein he
described her. The song of 'Bonny Chirsty' was
written after nearly seven years of wedded life. The
sentiments therein expressed speak better than com-
ment as to the happiness of Ramsay's marriage. One
verse of it may be quoted—

> ' How sweetly smells the simmer green !
>   Sweet taste the peach and cherry ;
> Painting and order please our een,
>   And claret makes us merry :
> But finest colours, fruits, and flowers,
>   And wine, though I be thirsty,
> Lose a' their charms and weaker powers,
>   Compared wi' those of Chirsty.'

About a year before his marriage, Ramsay had left
the shop in the Grassmarket, where he had commenced
business in 1707, and had established himself in the
High Street in premises already described, and which
exist to this day. There, under his sign of the 'Flying
Mercury,' he toiled and sang, and chatted and cracked
jokes with all and sundry, from sunrise to sunset, his wit
and his humour, and, as time rolled on, his poetic genius,
bringing many customers to his shop. Verily, a sunny-
souled man, in whom 'life with its carking cares' could
never extinguish his cheery *bonhomie* and self-confidence.

CHAPTER IV

RAMSAY's marriage was the turning-point of his career.
To him, as to every man who realises not alone the
moral but the social obligations he assumes when undertaking the holy charge of rendering a woman's life
happier and brighter than ever before, the responsi-
bilities of his new relation crystallised into the mould of
definite effort the energies hitherto diffused throughout
numberless diverse channels. Seldom has the philosophy
of wedded bliss been more felicitously stated than in his
Advice to Mr. —— on his Marriage. He remarks, as
though drawing on the fund of his own experience—

> ' Alake ! poor mortals are not gods,
> And therefore often fall at odds ;
> But little quarrels now and then,
> Are nae great faults 'tween wife and man.
> These help right often to improve
> His understanding, and her love.
> If e'er she take the pet, or fret,
> Be calm, and yet maintain your state ;
> An' smiling ca' her little foolie,
> Syne wi' a kiss evite a tulzie.
> This method's ever thought the braver
> Than either cuffs or *clish-ma-claver.*
> It shows a spirit low an' common
> That wi' ill-nature treats a woman.

41

They're of a make sae nice and fair
They maun be managed wi' some care;
Respect them they'll be kind an' civil,
But disregarded, prove the devil.'

But for another reason the year 1712 is as interesting
to us as students of his career as it was important to him.
In the early months of it he was introduced to the 'Easy
Club,' one of those politico - convivial societies that
sprang into existence early in the century, and were con-
spicuous features in the social customs of the period,
until its eighth and ninth decades, when, consequent
upon the expansion of the city north and south, the
tavern conviviality of 1740 was succeeded by the domestic
hospitality of 1790.

At the time of which we write, the capital of Scotland
was virtually represented by the one long street called
the High Street, or 'Edinburgh Street,' which crowned
the summit of the ridge extending from the Castle to
Holyrood Palace, the ancient home of the Stuarts.
From this main artery of traffic, smaller veins, in the
shape of narrow darksome closes, branched out, leading
to a second artery in the Cowgate, and to yet a third one
in the Grassmarket. During the panic that prevailed
after the Battle of Flodden, a wall of defence was drawn
around the town. By it the area of Edinburgh was
grievously circumscribed. Only what might be termed
the heart of the city was included, all lying beyond
falling within the anomalous designation of *suburbs*. For
two hundred years this seemingly impassable girdle
sternly checked the natural *overflow* of the city's life.
To reside outside the *ports* or gates was not only considered dangerous—it was unfashionable. And as there

was not accommodation for a tenth part of the inhabitants in the houses of two, or at most three, storeys which prevailed about the time of the Reformation, the architects of the Restoration period commenced the erection of those towering tenements, or *lands*,—twelve, fourteen, and even sixteen storeys high,—for which Edinburgh has been celebrated among the cities of Europe. Thus the families of the Scottish metropolis were packed together, one on the top of the other, like herrings in a barrel, in those quaint old houses, with their grim timber fronts, their crow-stepped gables and dormer windows, that remain even until to-day to show us the circumstances under which our fathers lived and loved.

In circumstances such as these, domestic comfort and the sweet seclusion of home were out of the question. So criminally overcrowded was the town that well-born gentlemen and their households were content with two or three rooms, wherein all the manifold duties of social and domestic life had to be performed. Robert Chambers, in his charming *Traditions of Edinburgh*, relates how the family of Mr. Bruce of Kennet, a leading lawyer, afterwards raised to the Bench, lived in a house of three rooms and a kitchen—a parlour, a con-sulting-room for Mr. Bruce, and a bedroom. The children, with their maid, had beds laid down for them at night in their father's room, the housemaid slept under the kitchen dresser, and the one man-servant was turned at night out of the house. Even a more striking example of the lack of accommodation was to be found in con-nection with the household arrangements of Mr. Kerr, the eminent goldsmith of Parliament Square, who 'stowed his *ménage* in a couple of small rooms above his booth-like shop, plastered against the wall of St. Giles Church; the nursery and kitchen, however, being in a cellar under the level of the street, where the children are said to have rotted off like sheep. . . . The town was, nevertheless, a funny, familiar, compact, and not unlikable place. Gentle and semple living within the compass of a single close, or even a single stair, knew and took an interest in each other.'

Such was the kind of home to which Allan Ramsay brought his bride. Two rooms, with a closet and a kitchen, for many a long year were the extent of their household accommodation. Such a state of things was not favourable to the development of the virtues purely domestic. Hence with Ramsay, as with other men, tavern life was accepted as a substitute for those comforts the sterner sex could not get at home. As Grant remarks in his *Old and New Edinburgh* : 'The slender house accommodation in the turnpike stairs compelled the use of taverns more than now. There the high-class advocate received his clients, and the physician his patients— each practitioner having his peculiar *howff*. There, too, gentlemen met in the evening for supper and conversation, without much expense, a reckoning of a shilling being a high one—so different then was the value of money and the price of viands.'

Mr. Logie Robertson, in his graphic and admirable introduction to the *Poems of Allan Ramsay* in the Canterbury Series, adds : 'Business lingered on all over the town to a much later period than is customary now, but by eight o'clock every booth was deserted and every shop closed, and the citizens for the most part gave themselves up to cheap conviviality and pastime for the next hour or two. Almost every tradesman had his favourite place in his favourite tavern, where, night after night, he cracked a quiet bottle and a canny joke before going home to his family. It was first business, then friendship ; and the claims of family after that.'

Out of this general spirit of conviviality arose those numberless Clubs wherein, upon the convivial stem, were graffed politics, literature, sport, science, as well as many other pursuits less worthy and less beneficial. No custom, no usage, no jest, in fact, seemed too trivial to be seized upon as the pretext to give a colour of excuse for founding a Club. Some of them were witty, others wise, others degrading. Such designations as the *Cape Club*,—so called from doubling the Cape of Leith Wynd, when half-seas over, to get home to the burgh of Low Calton, where several of the members lived ; the *Pious Club*, because the brethren met regularly to consume pies ; the *Spendthrift Club*, because no *habitué* was permitted to spend more than *fourpence halfpenny*, and others, were harmless in their way, and promoted a cheap *bonhomie* without leading the burghers into disgraceful excesses. But the *Hell-fire Club*, the *Sweating Club*, the *Dirty Club*, and others of a kindred order, were either founded to afford an opportunity for indulgence in riot and licence of every kind, or were intended to encourage habits as disgusting as they were brutal.

Not to be supposed is it that Ramsay had lived six-and-twenty years of his life without having practised, and we have no doubt enjoyed, the widespread conviviality of the period. Hence, though the Easy Club was the first of the social gatherings wherewith he actually informs us he was connected, we have no reason to doubt he had been associated with several of them before. In fact, in that poetical 'Essay' of his which stands first in the chronological order of composition, though not of publication, the *Elegy on Maggy Johnston*, who died anno 1711—an alewife whose little farm and hotel were situated in the village of Morningside, just beyond the Bruntsfield Links,—he seems to imply that a club of some kind met there. The third stanza runs as follows—

> ' And there by dizens we lay down ;
> Syne sweetly ca'd the healths aroun',
> To bonny lasses, black or brown,
> As we loo'd best :
> In bumpers we dull cares did drown,
> An' took our rest.'

But to the Easy Club[1] must be assigned the honour of having stimulated the nascent genius of the poet to achieve something that would convey to its members the fact that it was no ordinary tradesman who solicited admission into the charmed circle of the Society. James Ross, whose zeal for the poetic young wigmaker's social recognition was now materially increased, used all his influence to obtain for his son-in-law an *entrée* into the Club of which he was himself a member. Questionable, indeed, it is, when we consider the exclusive character of the association in question, the high social position of its members, and their avowed Jacobitical tenets, if even the influence of James Ross, powerful though it was, would alone have secured for Ramsay admission. But an inspiration, as happy as it was original, prompted him to embody his petition for admission into the Club in

[1]See Preface.

a poetical address. Such a course was of itself sufficient
to recommend him to men like Dr. Ruddiman and Dr.
Pitcairn. The poem, addressed to 'The Most Happy
Members of the Easy Club,' proceeded, in a felicitous
strain of gentle satire, blended with genial humour not
unlike Gay at his best, to plead his own cause why he
should be admitted as 'an *Easy* fellow.' His application was successful, and he was duly enrolled as a
member. The following lines extracted from it will
exhibit the character of the piece, which takes rank as
the earliest of his published poems—

> ' Were I but a prince or king,
>   I'd advance ye, I'd advance ye;
> Were I but a prince or king,
>   So highly I'd advance ye!
> Great wit and sense are ever found
> Among ye always to abound;
> Much like the orbs that still move round,
>   No ways constrained, but easy.
>   Were I but, etc.

> Most of what's hid from vulgar eye,
> Even from earth's centre to the sky,
> Your brighter thoughts do clearly spy,
>   Which makes you wise and easy.
>   Were I but, etc.

> All faction in the Church or State,
> With greater wisdom still you hate,
> And leave learn'd fools there to debate,—
>   Like rocks in seas you're easy.
>   Were I but, etc.

> I love ye well—O let me be
> One of your blythe Society;
> And like yourselves I'll strive to be
>   Aye humorous and easy.
>   Were I but, etc.

The benefits received by the self-confident young poet
were not alone of an intangible character.   Praise is an
excellent thing of itself, but a modicum of pudding along
with it is infinitely better.   To Ramsay the Easy Club
was the means of securing both.   The *rôle* of his literary
patrons was at once assumed by its members.   They
printed and published his *Address* at their own expense,
appointed him, within a few months' time, their ' Poet
Laureate,' and manifested, both by counsel and the
exercise of influence, the liveliest interest in his welfare.
No trivial service this to the youthful poet on the part
of his kindly club brethren.   How great it was, and how
decisive the effect of their generous championship in
establishing Ramsay's reputation on a sure basis, will
best be understood by glancing for a moment at the
character of the Easy Club and the *personnel* of its
membership.

Originally founded, under a different name, as a means
of frustrating, and afterwards of protesting against, the
Union, the Club, after its reconstruction in 1711, became
a Jacobite organisation pure and simple.   As Ramsay
himself stated in after years : ' It originated in the
antipathy we all of that day seemed to have at the ill-
humour and contradiction which arise from trifles,
especially those which constitute Whig and Tory, *without having the grand reason for it.*'   The grand reason
in question was the restoration of the Stuarts.   To give
a *soupçon* of mystery to their proceedings, as well as to
veil their identity when thus plotting against the ' powers
that be,' each member assumed a fictitious name,
generally that of some celebrated writer.   The poet, as
he himself relates, at first selected Isaac Beckerstaff,

suggestive of Steele and the *Tatler*. Eventually, however, he altered his *nom-de-guerre* to Gawain Douglas, one more in accordance with his patriotic sentiments.

The membership was limited to *twelve*, but at the time when Ramsay made his application we only know the names of five of those who belonged to it. Hepburn of Keith, in East Lothian, an antiquarian of no mean standing; Professor Pitcairn, late of Leyden, but at that time in the enjoyment of one of the largest practices as a physician in the Edinburgh of the period; Dr. Patrick Abercrombie, the eminent historian and antiquarian, author of *The Martial Achievements of the Scottish Nation*; Dr. Thomas Ruddiman, philologist, grammarian, printer, and librarian of the Advocates' Library,—one of the few Scottish polymaths over and above the Admirable Crichton and George Buchanan,—and James Ross the lawyer. Tradition has stated that Hamilton of Gilbertfield was also one of the 'Easy fellows,' as they dubbed themselves, but no confirmation of this fact could be discovered.

We reach now the commencement of Ramsay's literary career. For four years—in fact, until the breaking up of the Society after the Rebellion of 1715—all he wrote was issued with the *imprimatur* of the Easy Club upon it. That they were proud of him is evident from the statement made by Dr. Ruddiman in a letter to a friend: 'Our Easy Club has been increased by the admission of a young man, Ramsay by name, *sib* to the Ramsays of Dalhousie, and married to a daughter of Ross the writer. He will be heard tell o' yet, I'm thinking, or I am much out of my reckoning.'

The next pieces which our poet read to his patrons

4

were two he had written some time previous—to wit, a little Ode on the preservation from death by drowning of the son of his friend John Bruce, on August 19, 1710; and the *Elegy on Maggy Johnston*, the alewife, to which reference has already been made. The first of these bears evident traces of youth and inexperience, in both the esoteric and exoteric or technical mysteries of his art. For example, when referring to the danger wherein the lad and his companions had been placed, he remarks—

> ' Whilst, like the lamp's last flame, their trembling souls
> Are on the wing to leave their mortal goals ' ;

and he conjures up the following extraordinary spectacle of angelic gymnastics, whereby the rescue of the lads was effected—

> ' Angels came posting down the divine beam
> To save the helpless in their last extreme.'

Little promise was visible in that piece of future excellence, yet within eighteen months he had written the *Elegy on Maggy Johnston*, to which the critics of the Easy Club gave unstinted praise. For humorous description of the convivial habits of the day, and graphic word - painting, the poem is exceedingly happy. But alas ! judged by our latter-day standard of refinement, good taste, and morality, it is *caviare* to the general. Only to antiquarians and students of by-past customs do its allusions contain much that is either interesting or edifying.

To follow Ramsay's poetic development through all his earlier pieces would simply exhaust the interest of the reader. Suffice it to say, that, at the request of the

Easy Club, he wrote an Elegy on the death of Dr. Pitcairn in 1713, but the poem contained so many political references and satirical quips that he omitted it from the collected edition of his works in 1721. Pitcairn was a sort of Scottish Voltaire, a man far in advance of his time, who paid in popular suspicion and reprobation for his liberality and tolerance. What Robert Chambers remarks of him is well within the facts of the case. 'His sentiments and opinions on various subjects accord with the most enlightened views of the present day, and present a very striking and remarkable contrast to the ignorance and prejudice with which he was surrounded. Fanatics and bigots he detested, and by fanatics and bigots, as a matter of course, he was abused and calumniated. He was accused of being an atheist, a deist, a mocker and reviler of religion, . . . *and one who was twice drunk every day.*' Ramsay, in his *Elegy*, rebutted those grossly malevolent falsehoods, not only clearing the memory of his patron from such foul dishonour, but with bitingly sarcastic humour he turned the tables on the calumniators, by showing, over their action in connection with the Union, who in reality were the traitors.

To the instigation of the Easy Club we also owe the piece on *The Qualifications of a Gentleman,* published in 1715, subsequent to a debate in the Society on the subject. Ramsay versified the arguments used by the various speakers, executing the task in a manner at once so graceful and witty that the Club formally declared him to be 'a gentleman by merit.' Only a periphrastic method of signifying their approbation of his work was this, and did not imply any reflection upon his birth, as

might at first glance be supposed.   For in the concluding
lines of the poem Ramsay, with his genial *bonhomie* and
humour had said—

> ' Yet that we more good humour might display,
>   We frankly turned the vote another way ;
>   And in each thing we common topics shun,
>   So the great prize nor birth nor riches won.
>   The vote was carried thus :—that easy he
>   Who should three years a social fellow be,
>   And to our Easy Club give no offence,
>   After triennial trial, should commence
>   A gentleman ; which gives as just a claim
>   To that great title, as the blast of fame
>   Can give to those who tread in human gore.'

In 1715, also, he amused the members of the Club,
and after them the wits of Edinburgh, with some lines
on the current predictions regarding *The Great Eclipse
of the Sun*, foretold to take place during April 1715.
The following picture, descriptive of the awe and terror
produced on ignorant minds and on the brute creation
by the occurrence of the eclipse, is as pithily effective
in its simplicity and fidelity to life and nature as
anything in Crabbe's *Tales in Verse* or Shenstone's
Schoolmistress—

> ' When this strange darkness overshades the plains,
>   'Twill give an odd surprise to unwarned swains ;
>   Plain honest hinds, who do not know the cause,
>   Nor know of orbs, their motions or their laws,
>   Will from the half-ploughed furrows homeward bend
>   In dire confusion, judging that the end
>   Of time approacheth ; thus possessed with fear,
>   They'll think the gen'ral conflagration near.
>   The traveller, benighted on the road,
>   Will turn devout, and supplicate his God.

> Cocks with their careful mates and younger fry,
> As if 'twere evening, to their roosts will fly.
> The horned cattle will forget to feed,
> And come home lowing from the grassy mead.
> Each bird of day will to his nest repair,
> And leave to bats and owls the dusky air ;
> The lark and little robin's softer lay
> Will not be heard till the return of day.'

The years 1715–16 were evidently periods of great activity on Ramsay's part, for at least five other notable productions of his pen are to be assigned to that date. To him the revelation of his life's *métier* had at last come, and his enthusiasm in its prosecution was intense. Henceforward poetry was to represent to him the supreme aim of existence. But like the canny Scot he was, he preferred to regard its emoluments as a crutch rather than a staff; nay, on the other hand, the determination to discharge his daily duties in his trade, as he executed his literary labours, *con amore*, seems to have been ever present with him. On this point, and referring to his dual pursuits as a wigmaker and a poet, he writes to his friend Arbuckle—

> ' I theek the out, and line the inside
> Of mony a douce and witty pash,
> And baith ways gather in the cash.
>
> .   .   .   .   .   .
>
> Contented I have sic a skair,
> As does my business to a hair ;
> And fain would prove to ilka Scot,
> That pourtith's no the poet's lot.'

During the years in question Ramsay produced in rapid succession his poem *On Wit*, the Club being again responsible for this clever satire ; and also two humorous

Elegies, one on John Cowper, the Kirk-Treasurer's-Man, whose official oversight of the *nymphes de pave* furnished the poet with a rollickingly ludicrous theme, of which he made the most; the other, an *Elegy on Lucky Wood*, alewife in the Canongate, also gave Ramsay full scope for the exercise of that broad Rabelaisian humour, of his possession of which there was now no longer to be any doubt.

Finally, in 1716, he achieved his great success, which stamped him as unquestionably one of the greatest delineators that had as yet appeared, of rural Scottish life amongst the humbler classes. As is well known, a fragment is in existence consisting of one canto of a poem entitled *Christ's Kirk on the Green*. Tradition and internal evidence alike point to King James I. as the author. The theme is the description of a brawl at a country wedding, which breaks out just as the dancing was commencing. 'The king,' says Ramsay, 'having painted the rustic squabble with an uncommon spirit, in a most ludicrous manner, in a stanza of verse, the most difficult to keep the sense complete, as he had done, without being forced to bring in words for crambo's sake where they return so frequently, I have presumed to imitate His Majesty in continuing the laughable scene. Ambitious to imitate so great an original, I put a stop to the war, called a congress, and made them sign a peace, that the world might have their picture in the more agreeable hours of drinking, dancing, and singing. The following cantos were written, the one in 1715 (O.S. corresponding to January 1716), the other in 1718, about three hundred years after the first. Let no worthy poet despair of immortality,—good sense will always be the same in spite of the revolutions of fashion and the change of language.'

The task was no easy one, but Ramsay succeeded with remarkable skill in dovetailing the second and third cantos into the first, so that they read as the production of one mind. For faithful portraiture of Scottish rural manners, for a fidelity, even in the minutest details, recalling Teniers and his vividly realistic pictures of Dutch rustic life, the cantos are unrivalled in Scottish literature, save by the scenes of his own *Gentle Shepherd*.

CHAPTER V

RAMSAY'S fame as a poet, writing in the Scots vernacular,
was now thoroughly established. Though the patron-
age of the Easy Club could no longer be extended
to him, as the Government of the Elector of Hanover
—lately crowned King of England under the title of
George I.—had directed its suppression, the members
of it, while in a position to benefit him, had laid the
basis of his reputation so broad and deep that virtually
he had now only to build on their foundation.

He was distinctly the favourite of the 'auld wives' of
the town. In quarto sheets, familiarly known as *broadsides*, and similar to what had been hawked about the
country in his youth, his poems had hitherto been
issued. It became the fashion, when four o'clock arrived,
to send out their children, or their 'serving-lass,' with a
penny to procure Allan Ramsay's latest piece, in order
to increase the relish of their 'four-oors' Bohea' with
the broad humour of *John Cowper*, or *The Elegy upon
Lucky Wood*, or *The Great Eclipse*.

During the year or two immediately preceding the
publication of the quarto of 1721 this custom greatly

increased. Of course, a supply had to be forthcoming to meet such a demand, but of these, numberless pieces, on topics of political or merely ephemeral interest, were never republished after their appearance in *broadside* form. By an eminent collector of this species of literature the fact is stated, that there are considerably over two score of poems by Ramsay which have thus been allowed to slip into oblivion. Not that such a fate was undeserved. In many cases their indelicacy would debar their admission into any edition nowadays; in others, their lack of permanent general interest. Such subjects as *The Flytin' of Luckie Duff and Luckie Brown*, *A Dookin' in the Nor' Loch*, and *A Whiggish Lament*, were not the kind of themes his calmer and maturer judgment would care to contemplate being handed down to posterity as specimens of his work.

In 1719 Ramsay appears to have concluded, from the extensive sale his poems enjoyed even in *broadside* form, that the trade of a bookseller would not only be more remunerative than a wigmaker's, but would also be more in accord with his literary tastes and aspirations. For some months he had virtually carried on the two trades concurrently, his reputation undoubtedly attracting a large number of customers to his shop to have their wigs dressed by the popular poet of the day. But as his fame increased, so did his vanity. Of praise he was inordinately fond. ' Tell Allan he's as great a poet as Pope, and ye may get what ye like from him,' said the witty and outspoken Lord Elibank to a friend. The charge had more than a grain of truth in it. That man did not lack more than his share of self-complacent vanity who could write, as the vicegerent of great Apollo, as he informs us in *The Scribblers Lashed*, such lines as these—

> ' Wherefore pursue some craft for bread,
> Where hands may better serve than head ;
> Nor ever hope in verse to shine,
> Or share in Homer's fate or——'

Alas ! Allan, ' backwardness in coming forward ' was never one of thy failings !

To Allan, *digito monstrari* was a condition of things equivalent to the seventh heaven of felicity ; but he felt it would be more to his advantage to be pointed out as a bookseller than as a wigmaker, when his reputation as a poet would cause his social status to be keenly examined. We learn that he consulted his friend Ruddiman on the step, who spoke strongly in its favour, and gave him good sound advice as to the kind of stock most likely to sell readily. The 'Flying Mercury,' therefore, which up to this date had presided over the ' theeking ' of the *outside* of the 'pashes' (heads) of the worthy burgesses of Auld Reekie, was thereafter to preside, with even increased lustre, over the provision of material for lining the *inside* with learning and culture.

That the time was an anxious one for the poet there can be little doubt. He was virtually beginning the battle of life anew ; and though he did so with many advantageous circumstances in his favour, none the less was the step one to be undertaken only after the gravest consideration and calculation of probabilities. But by its results the change is shown to have been a wise one. From the outset the bookselling business proved a lucrative venture. The issue of his own *broadsides,* week by week, was of itself a considerable source of profit. These, in addition to being sold at his shop and hawked about the country, were disposed of on the streets of Edinburgh by itinerant stallkeepers, who were wont to regard the fact as one of great moment to themselves when they could cry, 'Ane o' Maister Ramsay's new poems—price a penny.' In this manner his famous piece, *The City of Edinburgh's Address to the Country*, was sown broadcast over the county.

Meantime, while Ramsay's literary and commercial prosperity was being established on so firm a basis, he was becoming quite a family man. The little house opposite Niddry's Wynd was gradually getting small enough for his increasing *ménage*. Since his marriage in 1712, happiness almost idyllic, as he records, had been his lot in his domestic relations. He had experienced the pure joy that thrills through a parent's heart on hearing little toddling feet pattering through his house, and sweet childish voices lisping the name 'father.' The following entries in the Register of Births and Baptisms for the City of Edinburgh speak for themselves :—

'At Edinburgh, 6th October 1713.

'Registrate to Allan Ramsay, periwige-maker, and Christian Ross, his spouse, New Kirk Parish—a son, Allan. Witnesses, John Symer, William Mitchell, and Robert Mein, merchant, burgesses ; and William Baxter.

'Registrate to Allan Ramsay, weegmaker, burges, and Christian Ross, his spouse, North East (College Kirk) Parish—a daughter named Susanna. Witnesses, John Symers, merchant, and John Morison, merchant. The child was born on the 1st instant. 3rd October 1714.

'Registrate to Allan Ramsay, weegmaker, and Christian Ross, his spouse, North East Parish — a son, Niell. Witnesses, Walter Boswell, sadler, and John Symer, merchant. 9th October 1715.

'Registrate to Allan Ramsay, weegmaker, and Christian Ross, his spouse, North East Parish—a son, Robert. Witnesses, John Symer, merchant, and Walter Boswell, sadler. The child was born on the 10th instant. 23rd November 1716.

'Registrate to Allan Ramsay, bookseller, and Christian Ross, his spouse — a daughter named Agnes. Witnesses, James Norie, painter, and George Young, chyrurgeon. Born the 9th instant. 10th August 1725.'

Besides these named above, Chalmers states that Christian Ross brought Allan Ramsay three other daughters, who were not recorded in the Register,—one born in 1719, one in 1720, and one in 1724,—who are mentioned in his letter to Smibert as 'fine girls, no ae wally-draigle among them all.'

In 1719 our poet published his first edition of 'Scots Songs,'—some original, others collected from all sources, and comprising many of the gems of Scottish lyrical poetry. The success attending the volume was instant and gratifying, and led, as we will see further on, to other publications of a cognate but more ambitious character. Almost contemporaneously was published, in a single sheet or *broadside*, what proved to be the germ of the *Gentle Shepherd*—to wit, a *Pastoral Dialogue between Patie and Roger*. The dialogue was reprinted in the quarto of 1721, and was much admired by all the lovers of poetry of the period.

A reliable gauge of the estimation wherein Ramsay was now held, as Scotland's great vernacular poet, is afforded in the metrical epistles sent to him during the closing months of 1719 by Lieutenant William Hamilton of Gilbertfield, to which Allan returned replies in similar terms. This was not a poetical tourney like the famous 'flyting' between Dunbar and Kennedy, two hundred and thirty years before. In the latter, the two tilters sought to say the hardest and the bitterest things of each other, though they professed to joust with pointless spears; in the former, Hamilton and Ramsay, on the contrary, vied each with the other in paying the pleasantest compliments. Gilbertfield contributed a luscious sop to his correspondent's vanity when he saluted him, in a stanza alluded to by Burns in his own familiar tribute, as—

> 'O fam'd and celebrated Allan !
> Renowned Ramsay ! canty callan !
> There's nowther Highland-man nor Lawlan,
>   In poetrie,
> But may as soon ding down Tantallan,
>   As match wi' thee.'

Then he proceeds to inform honest Allan that of 'poetry, the hail quintescence, thou hast suck'd up,' and affirms that—

> 'Tho' Ben and Dryden of renown
> Were yet alive in London town,
> Like kings contending for a crown,
>   'Twad be a pingle,
> Whilk o' you three wad gar words sound
>   And best to jingle.'

After such a glowing tribute, Allan could do no less than dip deep into his cask of compliments also, and assure

Gilbertfield that he felt taller already by this com-
mendation—

> 'When Hamilton the bauld and gay
>   Lends me a heezy,
> In verse that slides sae smooth away,
>   Well tell'd and easy.'

Then he proceeds to shower on his correspondent his
return compliments as follows—

> 'When I begoud first to cun verse,
> And could your "Ardry Whins" rehearse,
> Where Bonny Heck ran fast and fierce,
>   It warmed my breast;
> Then emulation did me pierce,
>   Whilk since ne'er ceast.'

Three epistles were exchanged on either side, bristling
with flattery, and with a little poetic criticism scattered
here and there. In Ramsay's second letter his irrepres-
sible vanity takes the bit in its teeth and runs away with
him. He appends a note with reference to his change
of occupation, as though he dreaded the world might
not know of it. 'The muse,' he says, 'not unreason-
ably angry, puts me here in mind of the favours she had
done by bringing me from stalking over bogs or wild
marshes, to lift my head a little brisker among the polite
world, which could never have been acquired by the low
movements of a mechanic.' He was a bookseller now,
of course, and could afford to look down on wigmakers
as base mechanics! His lovableness and generosity
notwithstanding, Ramsay's vanity and self-complacency
meets us at every turn. To omit mentioning it would
be to present an unfaithful portrait of the honest poet.
On the other hand, justice compels one to state that, if
vain, he was neither jealous nor ungenerous. He was

always ready to recognise the merits of others, and his egoism was not selfishness. Though he might not care to deny himself to his own despite for the good of others, he was perfectly ready to assist his neighbour when his own and his family's needs had been satisfied.

At this time, also, Sir William Scott of Thirlestane, Bart., a contemporary Latin poet, as Chalmers records, of no inconsiderable powers, hailed Ramsay as one of the genuine poets whose images adorned the temple of Apollo. In the 'Poemata D. Gulielmi Scoti de Thirle-stane,' printed along with the 'Selecta Poemata Archi-baldi Pitcarnii' (Edinburgh, 1727), the following lines occur—

> '*Effigies Allani Ramsæi, Poëtæ Scoti, inter cæteras Poëtarum Imagines in Templo Apollinis suspensa:*
>
> Ductam Parrhasiâ videtis arte
> Allani effigiem, favente Phœbo,
> Qui Scotos numeros suos, novoque
> Priscam restituit vigore linguam.
> Hanc Phœbus tabulam, hanc novem sorores
> Suspendunt lepidis jocis dicatam :
> Gaudete, O Veneres, Cupidinesque,
> Omnes illecebræ, facetiæque,
> Plausus edite ; nunc in æde Phœbi
> Splendet conspicuo decore, vestri
> Allani referens tabella vultus.'

As much as any other, this testimony evinces how rapidly our poet's reputation had increased.

At last, in the spring of 1720, Allan Ramsay came before the public, and challenged it to endorse its favourable estimate of his fugitive pieces by subscribing to a volume of his collected poems, 'with some new, not heretofore printed.' As Chambers remarks : 'The estimation in which the poet was now held was clearly

demonstrated by the rapid filling up of a list of subscribers, containing the names of all that were eminent
for talents, learning, or dignity in Scotland.' The
volume, a handsome quarto, printed by Ruddiman, and
ornamented by a portrait of the author, from the pencil
of his friend Smibert, was published in the succeeding
year, and the fortunate poet realised four hundred guineas
by the speculation. Pope, Steele, Arbuthnot, and Gay
were amongst his English subscribers.

The quarto of 1721 may be said to have closed
the youthful period in the development of Ramsay's
genius. Slow, indeed, was that development. He was
now thirty-five years of age, and while he had produced
many excellent pieces calculated to have made the name
of any mediocre writer, he had, as yet, given the world
nothing that could be classed as a work of genius. His
sketches of humble life and of ludicrous episodes occur-
ring among the lower classes in Edinburgh and the
rustics in the country, had pleased a wide *clientéle* of
readers, because they depicted with rare truth and
humour, scenes happening in the everyday life of the
time. But in no single instance, up to this date, had
he produced a work that would live in the minds of the
people as expressive of those deep, and, by them, in-
communicable feelings that go to the composition of
class differences.

As a literary artist, Ramsay was destined to develop
into a *genre* painter of unsurpassed fidelity to nature.
As yet, however, that which was to be the distinctive
characteristic of his pictures had not dawned upon his
mind. But the time was rapidly approaching. Already
the first glimmerings of apprehension are to be detected

in his tentative endeavours to realise his *métier* in the pastoral dialogue of *Patie and Roger* republished in his volume.

The quarto of 1721 contained, moreover, several pieces that had not been previously printed. These we will at present only mention *en passant*, reserving critical analysis for our closing chapters. Not the least noticeable of the poems in the volume are those wherein he lays aside his panoply of strength,—the 'blythe braid Scots,' or vernacular,—and challenges criticism on what he terms 'his English poems.' These were undoubtedly the most ambitious flights in song hitherto attempted by the Scottish Tityrus. To the study of Dryden, Cowley, Swift, Pope, and Arbuthnot, he had devoted himself,— particularly to Pope's translation of Homer's *Iliad*, and to the collected edition of the works of the great author of the *Rape of the Lock*, issued in 1717. He had been in correspondence for some years previous with several of the leading English poets of the day, and with other individuals well known both in politics and London society, such as Josiah Burchet, who, when he died in 1746, had been Secretary to the Admiralty for forty-five years, and had sat in six successive Parliaments. This was the friend whose admiration for Ramsay was so excessive as to prompt him to send (as was the custom of the time) certain recommendatory verses for insertion in the quarto, wherein he hailed honest Allan in the following terms—

> 'Go on, famed bard, the wonder of our days,
> And crown thy head with never-fading bays;
> While grateful Britons do thy lines revere,
> And value as they ought their Virgil here.'

5

Small wonder is it that, stimulated by such flattery, Allan should have desired to evince to his friends by the Thames, that the notes of their northern brother of the lyre were not confined to the humble strains of his own rustic reed.

In the quarto, therefore, we have a poem, *Tartana, or The Plaid*, written in heroic couplets, with the avowed desire to reinstate in popular favour the silken plaid, which, from time immemorial, had been the favourite attire of Scots ladies, but, since the Rebellion of 1715, had been somewhat discarded, in consequence of Whiggish prejudices that it was a badge of disloyalty to the reigning house. Then we have *Content*, a long piece of moral philosophy in verse, and the *Morning Interview*, a poem written under the spell of Pope's *Rape of the Lock*, wherein the very machinery of the sylphs is copied from the great English satire. Nor is the 'South Sea Bubble,' which ran its brief course from 1718 to 1720, forgotten in *Wealth, or The Woody* (gallows), and two shorter poems illustrative of the prevailing madness. Epigrams, Addresses, Elegies, and Odes are also included, along with one or two of his famous poetical *Epistles*, modelled on those of Horace, and brimming over with genial *bonhomie* and good-humoured epicureanism. In this volume, also, we have additional evidence afforded how fondly he had become attached to Edinburgh and its environs. Scarce a poem is there in the book that lacks some reference to well-known features in the local landscape, showing that he still retained the love of wandering, in his spare hours, amid Pentland glens and by fair Eskside. Only with one extract will the reader's patience be taxed here. It is from his *Ode to the Ph—*, and is obviously an imitation of Horace's Ode to Thaliarchus. All the sunny glow of the great Roman's genius seems reflected in this revival of his sentiments, albeit under varying physical conditions, well-nigh three hundred and fifty *lustra* afterwards. The lines cleave to the memory with a persistence that speaks volumes for the catholicity and appropriateness of the thoughts—

'Look up to Pentland's tow'ring tap,
    Buried beneath big wreaths o' snaw,
O'er ilka cleugh, ilk scaur, and slap,
    As high as ony Roman wa'.

Driving their ba's frae whins or tee,
    There's no ae gowfer to be seen ;
Nor doucer fouk, wysing a-jee
    The biassed bowls on Tamson's green.

Then fling on coals, and ripe the ribs,
    And beek the house baith butt and ben ;
That mutchkin stoup it hauds but dribs,
    Then let's get in the tappit hen.

Guid claret best keeps out the cauld,
    An' drives awa' the winter soon :
It makes a man baith gash and bauld,
    An' heaves his saul ayont the moon.

Leave to the gods your ilka care ;
    If that they think us worth their while,
They can a rowth o' blessings spare,
    Which will our fashous fears beguile.'

CHAPTER VI

THE popularity accruing to Ramsay from the publication of the quarto of 1721 was so great that
his fame was compared, in all seriousness, with that
of his celebrated English contemporaries, Pope, Swift
and Addison. No better evidence of the unfitness of
contemporary opinion to gauge the real and ultimate
position of any author in the hierarchy of genius could
be cited than the case now before us. The critical
perspective is egregiously untrue. The effect of person-
ality and of social qualities is permitted to influence a
verdict that should be given on the attribute of intellectual excellence alone. Only through the lapse of
time is the personal equation eliminated from the
estimate of an author's relative proportion to the
aggregate of his country's genius.

Nor were his countrymen aware of the extravagance
of their estimate when such a man as Ruddiman styled
him 'the Horace of our days,' and when Starrat,
in a poetical epistle, apostrophises him in terms like
these—

' Ramsay! for ever live; for wha like you,
   In deathless sang, sic life-like pictures drew?

Not he wha whilome wi' his harp could ca'
The dancing stanes to big the Theban wa';
Nor he (shame fa's fool head!) as stories tell,
Could whistle back an auld dead wife frae hell.'

James Clerk of Penicuik considered Homer and Milton to be the only worthy compeers of the Caledonian bard; and Sir William Bennet of Marlefield insisted the Poet-Laureateship should be conferred on Ramsay, as the singer who united in himself the three great qualifications—genius, loyalty, and *respectability !* Certainly honest Allan would have been a Triton amongst such minnows as Nicholas Rowe, who held the bays from 1714 – 18, or Laurence Eusden, whose tenure of the office lasted from 1718 to 1730, but of whose verse scarce a scrap remains.

Compliments reached Ramsay from all quarters of the compass. Burchet, Arbuckle, Aikman, Arbuthnot, Ambrose Philips, Tickell, and many others, put on record their appreciation of his merits as a poet. But of all the testimonies, that which reached him from Pope was the most valued, and drew from Allan the following lines, indicative of his intense gratification, while also forming a favourable example of his skill in epigram—

' Three times I've read your Iliad o'er:
  The first time pleased me well;
New beauties unobserved before,
  Next pleased me better still.

Again I tried to find a flaw,
  Examined ilka line;
The third time pleased me best of a',
  The labour seem'd divine.

Henceforward I'll not tempt my fate,
On dazzling rays to stare;
Lest I should tine dear self-conceit
And read and write nae mair.'

His position in Edinburgh society was greatly im-
proved by the success of the volume. The magnates
of 'Auld Reekie' who still clung to the capital their
forefathers had loved,—the legal luminaries of Bench and
Bar, the Professors of the University, the great medicos
of the town,—all were proud to know the one man who
was redeeming the Scottish poetry of that age from the
charge of utter sterility. There was the Countess of
Eglinton, 'the beautiful Susannah Kennedy of the
house of Colzean,' whose 'Eglinton air' and manners
in society were, for half a century, regarded as the models
for all young maidens to imitate. Living as she did
until 1780, when she had attained the great age of
ninety-one, she was visited by Dr. Johnson during his
visit to Scotland in 1773. On that occasion it transpired
that the Countess had been married before the lexico-
grapher was born; whereupon, says Grant, 'she smartly
and graciously said to him that she might have been his
mother, and now adopted him; and at parting she
embraced him, a mark of affection and condescension
which made a lasting impression on the mind of the
great literary bear.' She was one of Ramsay's warmest
admirers. Then there were Lord Stair and his lovely
lady, Duncan Forbes of Culloden, then about to become
Lord Advocate: also, Laurence Dundas, Professor of
Humanity; Colin Drummond, of Metaphysics; William
Law, of Moral Philosophy; Alexander Monro (*primus*),
of Anatomy, and George Preston, of Botany, all of the

University of Edinburgh—and all deeply interested in the quaint, cheery, practical-minded little man, who combined in himself the somewhat contradictory qualities of an excellent poet and a keen man of business. Thus the influence was a reciprocal one. His poetry attracted customers to his shop, while his bookselling in turn brought him in contact with social celebrities, whose good offices the self-complacent poet would not suffer to be lost for lack of application.

In 1722 the proprietor of the famous John's Coffee House and Tavern, in Parliament Close, off the High Street,—which, by the way, still exists,—was a man named Balfour. The latter, who had lived for some time in London, had acquired a smattering of literary culture, and conceived the idea of rendering his house the Edinburgh counterpart of Will's or Button's. He set himself to attract all the leading wits and men of letters in the Scottish metropolis at the time, and speedily raised his house to considerable celebrity during the third and fourth decades of last century. To Allan Ramsay he paid especial court, and the poet became a daily visitor at the tavern. Here he would meet many of the judges and leading lawyers, the professors from the College, any visitors of note who might be in town; also Clerk of Penicuik, Sir William Bennet of Marlefield, Hamilton of Bangour, the poet, Preston and Crawford, the rising young song-writers of the day, as well as Beau Forrester, the leader of fashion in Edinburgh, who is recorded to have exhibited himself, once at least, in an open balcony in a chintz nightgown, and been dressed and powdered by his *valet de chambre* as an object-lesson to the town dandies how to get themselves up. There, too, among

many others, he probably met the famous, or rather infamous, John Law of Lauriston, banker, financier, and
cheat, who was in Edinburgh in 1722, after having
brought France to the verge of bankruptcy and ruined
thousands by his financial schemes. A motley crowd,
in good sooth; yet one whence our poet could draw
many a hint for future use.

The success of the quarto encouraged Ramsay to
redoubled efforts, and the next six or seven years are the
period of his greatest literary fertility. In 1722 appeared
his *Fables and Tales* and *The Three Bonnets*, a poem in
four cantos. In some criticisms of Ramsay the statement has been made that he owed the idea of his *Fables*
to Gay's inimitable collection. That this is an error is
evident, seeing the latter did not publish his volume
until 1726. In his preface to the *Fables and Tales* the
poet says: 'Some of the following are taken from
Messieurs la Fontaine and La Motte, whom I have
endeavoured to make speak Scots with as much ease as
I can; at the same time aiming at the spirit of these
eminent authors without being too servile a translator.'
Ramsay took as his prototypes in this species of composition, Phaedrus, La Fontaine, and Desbillons, rather
than Æsop. Many of the incidents he drew from
occurrences in the everyday life around him. For
example, *Jupiter's Lottery* has obvious reference to the
South Sea Bubble lotteries; while *The Ass and the Brock*
was thought at the time to be a sly skit on the addle-pated
Commissioners Walpole had that year sent up to Scotland to nip northern Jacobitism in the bud.

Ramsay's *Tales* in verse contain some of his daintiest
though not his strongest work. He makes no claim to

originality with respect to them, but admits they are drawn in many cases from La Motte and other sources. In his preface he says : ' If my manner of expressing a design already invented have any particularity that is agreeable, good judges will allow such imitations to be originals formed upon the idea of another. Others, who drudge at the dull verbatim, are like timorous attendants, who dare not move one pace without their master's leave.' Some of the *Tales* are obviously modelled on those of Chaucer and Boccaccio, but in most of his, he insinuates a political or social moral, while they narrate the story for the story's sake. *The Three Bonnets* is a satire on his countrymen for being so shortsighted, in their own interests, as to consent to the Union. Bristle, the eldest of the three brothers in the tale, was intended to represent the Tories and Scots Jacobites, who were opposed to the scheme, and he is therefore drawn as a man of great resolution and vigour of character. Bawsy, the youngest, or weak brother, shadowed forth the character of those who consented under the persuasion of the nobility ; while Joukum, the second eldest of the trio,—a vicious, dissipated *roué*,—stood for the portrait of those Scots noblemen who accepted Lord Somers' bribes, and sold their country to the English alliance. The story ran that their father, Duniwhistle, on his deathbed, had, to each of the brothers, presented a bonnet with which they were never to part. If they did so, ruin would overtake them. Joukum falls in love with Rosie, a saucy quean, who demands, as the price of her hand, that he should beg, borrow, or steal for her the three bonnets. Joukum proceeds to Bristle, and receives a very angry reception ; he next repairs to lazy Bawsy, who, dazzled by the promises the other makes as to the good things he will receive after the wedding, surrenders his bonnet, which Joukum lays with his own at the feet of Rosie. The latter agrees to wed Joukum, and a vivid picture is drawn of the neglected state of poor Bawsy after this is accomplished. Rosie proves a harridan, leading Joukum a sorry dance ; and the poem concludes with the contrasted pictures of the contented prosperity of Bristle—Scotland as she might have been had she not entered the Union—and the misery of Bawsy, representing Scotland as she then was. Somewhat amusing is it to conjecture what Ramsay's feelings would be on this subject could he for an instant be permitted to witness the progress of Scotland during the past hundred and thirty years, and the benefits that have accrued to her from the Union.

Amongst his metrical tales, one of the finest, without question, is *The Lure*, a satirical fable or allegory, whereof the moral, as may best be stated in the poet's own words—

> ——'shews plainly,
> That carnal minds attempt but vainly
> Aboon this laigher warld to mount,
> While slaves to Satan.'

The narrative, however, though possessing many merits, is too indelicate for latter-day taste even to be sketched in outline.

In 1723 appeared his poem *The Fair Assembly*, directed against the Puritanic severity of that section of the community which took exception to dancing and such pleasant amusements, alike for young and old. Nothing reveals to us more vividly the strange contrasts in the

religious life of the time, than the fact that the clergy
winked at the drunkenness which was so prominent a
feature in the social customs of the eighteenth century,
and fulminated unceasingly against dancing. Those
who indulged in it were in many instances barred from
sacramental privileges, and had such pleasant epithets
as 'Herodias' and 'Jezebel' hurled at them. As
Chambers states in his *Traditions of Edinburgh* :
'Everything that could be called public or promiscuous
amusement was held in abhorrence by the Presbyterians,
and only struggled through a desultory and degraded
existence by the favour of the Jacobites, who have
always been a less strait-laced part of the community.
Thus there was nothing like a conventional system of
dancing in Edinburgh till the year 1710,' when at length
—induced, probably, by the ridicule cast on the ascetic
strictness of Scottish social functions by the English
visitors who from time to time sojourned in 'the grey
metropolis of the north'—a private association commenced
weekly *réunions*, under the name of 'The Assembly.'
Its first rooms, according to Arnot's *History of Edinburgh*,
were in a humble tenement in the West Bow (standing
on the site now occupied by St. John's Free Church),
where they continued to be located until 1720, when
they were removed to Old Assembly Close. In the
West Bow days it was, as Jackson tells us in his
History of the Stage, that the Presbyterian abhorrence of
'promiscuous dancing' once rose to such a height
that a crowd of people attacked the rooms when an
'Assembly' was being held, and actually perforated the
closed doors with red-hot spits.

As affording an interesting picture of the austerity of

the time, a sentence or two may be quoted from a little pamphlet in the Advocates' Library entitled, 'A Letter from a Gentleman in the Country to his Friend in the City, with an Answer thereto concerning the New Assembly.' The author writes : 'I am informed there is lately a Society erected in your town which I think is called an "Assembly." The speculations concerning this meeting have of late exhausted the most part of the public conversation in this countryside. Some are pleased to say 'tis only designed to cultivate polite conversation and genteel behaviour among the better sort of folks, and to give young people an opportunity of accomplishing themselves in both ; while others are of opinion it will have quite a different effect, and tends to vitiate and deprave the minds and inclinations of the younger sort.'

The Assemblies themselves must have been characterised by the most funereal solemnity, particularly during the *régime* of the famous 'Mistress of Ceremonies,' or directress, Miss Nicky Murray. So late as 1753, when the horror at 'promiscuous dancing' might be supposed to have mitigated a little, Goldsmith, who then visited the Assembly, relates that, on entering the room, he saw one end of it 'taken up by the ladies, who sat dismally in a group by themselves. On the other side stand their pensive partners that are to be, but with no more intercourse between the sexes than between two countries at war. The ladies, indeed, may ogle and the gentlemen sigh, but an embargo is laid on any closer commerce.'

As might well be supposed, such bigoted austerity had no friend in Allan Ramsay. All that he could do he did to dissipate the mistaken ideas of the Scottish clergy and the stricter section of the Presbyterian Church, on the subject of dancing and the holding of the Assemblies. In the preface to his poem of *The Fair Assembly* he remarks : ' It is amazing to imagine that any are so destitute of good sense and manners as to drop the least unfavourable sentiment against the Assembly. It is to be owned with regret, the best of things have been abused. The Church has been, and in many countries is, the chief place for assignations that are not warrantable. . . . The beauty of the fair sex, which is the great preserver of harmony and society, has been the ruin of many. So places designed for healthful and mannerly dancing have, by people of an unhappy turn, been debauched by introducing gaming, drunkenness, and indecent familiarities. But will any argue from these we must have no churches, no wine, no beauties, no literature, no dancing ? Forbid it, Heaven ! whatever is under your auspicious conduct must be improving and beneficial in every respect.'

His poem is an ode in praise of dancing, and of the manner in which the Assemblies were conducted. Fortifying his case with Locke's well-known sentence— ' Since nothing appears to me to give children so much becoming confidence and behaviour, and so raise them to the conversation of those above their age, as dancing, I think they should be taught to dance as soon as they are capable of learning it,' he boldly avows himself as an advocate for the moderate indulgence in the amusement, both as health - giving and as tending to improve the mind and the manners, and concludes with these two spirited stanzas, which are quoted here as space will not permit us to refer to the piece again—

> ' Sic as against the Assembly speak,
>   The rudest sauls betray,
> Where matrons, noble, wise, and meek,
>   Conduct the healthfu' play.
> Where they appear, nae vice dare keek,
>   But to what's good gives way ;
> Like night, soon as the morning creek
>   Has ushered in the day.
>
> Dear Em'brugh ! shaw thy gratitude,
>   And of sic friends make sure,
> Wha strive to make our minds less rude,
>   And help our wants to cure ;
> Acting a generous part and good,
>   In bounty to the poor ;
> Sic virtues, if right understood,
>   Should ev'ry heart allure.'

But we must hasten on. In 1724 Ramsay published his poem on *Health*, inscribed to the Earl of Stair, and written at the request of that nobleman. In it Ramsay exhibits his full powers as a satirist, and inculcates the pursuit of health by the avoidance of such vices as sloth, effeminacy, gluttony, ebriety, and debauchery, which he personifies under the fictitious characters of Cosmelius, Montanus, Grumaldo, Phimos, Macro, etc. These were said to be drawn from well-known Edinburgh *roués* of the time, and certainly the various types are limned and contrasted with a masterly hand. To the cultured reader, this is the poem of all Ramsay's minor works best calculated to please and to convey an idea of his style, though at times his genius seems to move under constraint.

But in 1724 our poet showed himself ambitious of winning distinction in a new field. In 1718, as was stated previously, he had published a volume of *Scots Songs*, some of them original, but a large number of them adapted from older and imperfect copies. So successful had the venture been, that a second edition had been called for in 1719, and a third in 1722. To attempt something of a cognate character, yet upon a larger scale, Ramsay now felt encouraged. In January 1724 appeared the first volume of the *Tea-table Miscellany: a Collection of Scots Sangs*. The second volume was published in 1725, with the note by Ramsay: 'Being assured how acceptable new words to known good tunes would prove, I engaged to make verses for above sixty of them in these two volumes; about thirty were done by some ingenious young gentlemen, who were so pleased with my undertaking that they generously lent me their assistance.' 'Among those young gentlemen,' as Professor Masson says in his excellent monograph on Ramsay in his *Edinburgh Sketches and Memories*, 'we can identify Hamilton of Bangour, young David Malloch (afterwards Mallet), William Crawford, William Walkinshaw,' to which we would add James Preston. A third volume of the *Miscellany* appeared in 1727 and a fourth in 1732, though, as regards the last, grave doubts exist whether Ramsay were really its editor or collector. Few compilations have ever been more popular. In twenty-five years twelve large editions were exhausted, and since Ramsay's death several others have seen the light, some better, some worse, than the original. All classes in the community were appealed to by the songs contained in the *Miscellany*. That he

intended such to be the case is evident from the first
four lines of his dedication, in which he offers the
contents—

> 'To ilka lovely British lass,
>   Frae ladies Charlotte, Anne, and Jean,
> Down to ilk bonny singing Bess,
>   Wha dances barefoot on the green.'

In the collection each stratum of society finds the songs
wherewith it had been familiar from infancy to age.
Tunes that were old as the days of James V. were
wedded to words that caught the cadences of the music
with admirable felicity ; words, too, had tunes assigned
them which enabled them to be sung in castle and cot,
in hall and hut, throughout 'braid Scotland.' The
denizens of fashionable drawing-rooms found their
favourites—'Ye powers ! was Damon then so blest ?'
'Gilderoy,' 'Tell me, Hamilla ; tell me why'—in these
fascinating volumes, even as the Peggies and the Jennies
of the ewe-bughts and the corn-rigs rejoiced to note that
'Katy's Answer,' 'Polwart on the Green,' 'My Daddy
forbad, my Minny forbad,' and 'The Auld Gudeman,'
had not been lost sight of. For many a long day, at
each tea-party in town, or rustic gathering in the country,
the *Tea-Table Miscellany* was in demand, or the songs
taken from it, for the entertainment of those assembled.

The widespread delight evoked by the *Miscellany*
allured Ramsay to essay next a task for which, it must
be confessed, his qualifications were scanty. Nine
months after the publication of the first volume of the
Miscellany—to wit, in October 1724—appeared another
compilation, *The Evergrene : being ane Collection of Scots
Poems, wrote by the Ingenious before* 1600. It was dedi-

cated to the Duke of Hamilton, and in the dedicatory epistle he informs his Grace that 'the following old bards present you with an entertainment that can never be disagreeable to any Scotsman. . . . They now make a demand for that immortal fame that tuned their souls some hundred years ago. They do not address you with an indigent face and a thousand pitiful apologies to bribe the goodwill of the critics. No ; 'tis long since they were superior to the spleen of these sour gentle-men.' He had been granted access to the 'Bannatyne MSS.' — the literary remains of George Bannatyne, poet, antiquarian, and collector of ancient manuscripts of Scottish poetry. This valuable repository of much that otherwise would have perished was lent to Ramsay by the Hon. William Carmichael of Skirling, advocate (brother to the Earl of Hyndford), with permission to extract what he required. From this priceless treasure-trove he drew specimens of Dunbar, Henryson, Alexander Scott, Lyndsay, Kennedy, Montgomery, Sempill, Gavin Douglas, and others. A similar favour was in 1770 granted to Lord Hailes when preparing his volume, *Ancient Scottish Poems*. Interesting, therefore, it is, to compare the manner in which the two editors respect-ively fulfilled their tasks.

In Ramsay's case the poems he selected from the Bannatyne MSS. were passed through the alembic of his own brain. Everything was sacrificed to popularity and intelligibility. Lord Hailes, on the other hand, was the most scrupulous of editors, refusing to alter a single letter ; for, as he said, the value of the poems lies in the insight they afford us into the state of the language at the periods when the various pieces were written.

6

Alter them in any degree, even the slightest, and you destroy the intrinsic character of the composition. 'In making his compilation from the Bannatyne MSS.,' continued Lord Hailes, 'Ramsay has omitted some stanzas and added others, has modernised the versification and varied the ancient mode of spelling.' To offend thus was to render himself liable to the severest censure from all literary antiquarians. The fault was as inexcusable as would be a trader's in palming off shoddy goods as those of the best materials. As an example of the ruthless liberties our poet took with the text, it may be well to follow Chalmers' example, and print side by side a stanza of Ramsay's 'paraphrase' and Lord Hailes' severely accurate rendering of the opening of Dunbar's 'Thistle and the Rose'—

Ramsay.
'Quhen Merch with variand winds was overpast,
    And sweet Apryle had with his silver showers
Tane leif of Nature with an orient blast,
    And lusty May, that mudder is of flowrs,
    Had maid the birds begin the tymous hours ;
Amang the tendir odours reid and quhyt,
Quhois harmony to heir was grit delyt.'

Hailes.
'Quhen Merche wes with variand windis past,
    And Appryll had with her silver shouris
Tane leif at Nature with ane orient blast,
    And lusty May, that mudder is of flouris,
    Had maid the birdis to begyn thair houris
Amang the tendir odouris reid and quhyt,
Quhois harmony to heir it wis delyt.'

In Dunbar's 'Lament for the Deth of the Makkaris' he not only varied but added several lines, and these in the silliest manner possible. For example, at the

conclusion of Dunbar's noble elegy, Ramsay must needs
tack on three stanzas, as a prophecy by Dunbar himself,
wherein the vanity-full poet is introduced as 'a lad frae
Hethermuirs.' What censure could be too strong for
inappropriate fooling like the following, coming in to
mar the solemn close of Dunbar's almost inspired lines ?—

> ' Suthe I forsie, if spaecraft had,
> Frae Hether-muirs sall rise a lad,
> Aftir two centries pas, sall he
> Revive our fame and memorie :
>
> Then sal we flourish *evirgrene* ;
> All thanks to careful Bannatyne,
> And to the patron kind and frie
> Wha lends the lad baith them and me.
>
> Far sall we fare baith eist and west,
> Owre ilka clime by Scots possest ;
> Then sen our warks sall never dee,
> *Timor mortis non turbat me.*'

In the *Evergreen* Ramsay published two of his own
poems, *The Vision* (in which the author bewails the
Union and the banishment of the Stuarts) and *The
Eagle and the Robin Reid - breist* (likewise a Jacobite
poem), wilfully altering the spelling in both, and introducing archaicisms into the thought, so as to pass them
off as 'written by the ingenious before 1600.' He also
inserted *Hardyknute*, a fragment, which subsequent
research has proved to have been written by Lady
Elizabeth Wardlaw, a contemporary of Ramsay's.
Although the *Evergreen* did much to revive popular
interest in early Scottish poetry, and thus prepare the
way for Lord Hailes and Bishop Percy, from a critical
point of view it was worse than worthless, inasmuch as

many of the errors and alterations appearing in Ramsay's specimens of our early Scots literary remains, have not been corrected even to this day.

But though Ramsay, in the estimation of stern literary antiquarians, has been guilty of an offence so heinous,—an offence vitiating both the *Tea-Table Miscellany* and the *Evergreen*,—on the other hand, from the point of view of the popular reader, his action in modernising the language, at least, was not only meritorious but necessary, if the pieces were to be intelligible to the great mass of the people. Remembered, too, it must be, that Ramsay lived before the development of what may be styled the antiquarian 'conscience,' in whose code of literary morality one of the cardinal commandments is, 'Thou shalt in no wise alter an ancient MS., that thy reputation and good faith may be unimpugned in the land wherein thou livest, and that thou mayest not bring a nest of critical hornets about thine ears.'

In his *Reminiscences of Old Edinburgh*, Dr. Daniel Wilson thus succinctly states the case : 'Ramsay had much more of the poet than the antiquary in his composition ; and had, moreover, a poet's idea of valuing verse less on account of its age than its merit. He lived in an era of literary masquerading and spurious antiques, and had little compunction in patching and eking an old poem to suit the taste of his Edinburgh customers.' He was no Ritson,—and, after all, even Plautus had, for three hundred years after the revival of learning, to await his Ritschl !

CHAPTER VII

'THE GENTLE SHEPHERD'; SCOTTISH IDYLLIC POETRY;
RAMSAY'S PASTORALS—1725-30

In the quarto of 1721, not the least remarkable of
its contents had been two Pastoral Dialogues, the
one between Richy (Sir Richard Steele) and Sandy
(Alexander Pope), and based on the death of Addison :
the other between Patie and Roger, and concerning
itself solely with a representation of rural life. Amongst
the best pieces in the volume both undoubtedly ranked.
In 1723 appeared another metrical dialogue, *Jenny and
Meggy*, betraying obvious kinship with *Patie and Roger*.
So delighted were his friends, the Clerks and the Bennets,
Professors Drummond and Maclaurin, and many others,
with the *vraisemblance* to Scottish rural life, and with
the true rustic flavour present in the two dialogues, that
they entreated him to add some connecting links, and to
expand them into a pastoral drama. Doubtful of his
ability to execute a task demanding powers so varied,
and so supreme, Ramsay for a time hesitated. But at
length, induced by their advice, he threw himself into the
undertaking with enthusiasm. In a letter to his kinsman
William Ramsay of Templehall, dated April 8, 1724, he
writes : " I am this vacation going through with a
Dramatick Pastoral, whilk I design to carry the length of

five acts, in verse a' the gate, and, if I succeed according
to my plan, I hope to tope [rival] with the authors of
Pastor Fido and *Aminta*.'

On the scenes wherewith he had become acquainted
during his manifold rambles over the hills and the vales,
the glens and glades, of fair Midlothian, he now drew, as
well as from the quaint and curious types of character—
the Symons, the Glauds, the Bauldies, the Rogers, the
Madges, and the Mauses—wherewith he had come into
contact during such seasons. That he stinted either time
or trouble in making the drama as perfect as possible is
evident from the prolonged period over which its composition was spread, and the number of drafts he made
of it. Some of the songs, he informed Sir David Forbes,
had been written no fewer than six times. At length,
early in July 1725, prefaced by a dedication in prose
from himself to the Right Hon. Susannah, Countess of
Eglinton, and by a poetical address to the same beautiful
patroness, from the pen of William Hamilton of Bangour,
the poet, *The Gentle Shepherd* made its appearance.

Its success from the very outset was unparalleled in
Scottish literature up to that date. It seemed literally to
take the country by storm. By all ranks and classes, by
titled ladies in their boudoirs, as well as by milkmaids
tripping it to the bughts with leglins and pails, the poem
was admiringly read, and its songs sung. Its performance
on the stage in 1726, only served to whet the public
appetite. By the leading poets of the day, Pope, Swift,
Gay, Tickell, Ambrose Philips, and Lord Lansdowne, as
well as by the most influential critics, Dennis, Theobald,
and Dr. Ruddiman, the work was hailed as one of the
most perfect examples of the pastoral that had appeared

since the *Idylls* of Theocritus. No less eminent a judge of poetry than Alexander Pope considered it in many respects superior to the *Shepherds' Calendar*; while Gay was so enthusiastic in his admiration that he sent the work over to Swift, with the remark, 'At last we have a dramatic pastoral, though it *is* by a Scot.'

The first edition of *The Gentle Shepherd* was exhausted in a few months, and in January 1726 Ruddiman printed the second, while the third and a cheaper one was called for towards the close of the same year. The enormous sale of the poem may be estimated by the fact that the tenth edition was printed in 1750 by R. & A. Foulis of Glasgow. So great was the accession of popularity accruing to Ramsay through the publication of *The Gentle Shepherd*, and so rapid the increase in his book-selling business, that he found it absolutely necessary to shift his place of business, or *Scotice dictu*, to 'flit' to larger premises, in the first storey of the eastern gable-end of the Luckenbooths, a block of towering *lands* or tenements which, until 1817, stood in the very centre of the High Street, obstructing the thoroughfare, and affording a curious commentary on the expedients to which the burgesses of Edinburgh were compelled to resort, to eke out to the utmost the space enclosed within the charmed circle of the Flodden Wall.

At his 'flitting,' also, he changed his sign, and, thinking the 'Flying Mercury' no longer applicable to his new pursuits, he adopted the heads of Ben Jonson and Drummond of Hawthornden, a sign which in local parlance gradually grew to bear the title of 'The Twa Heids.' In his new premises also, Ramsay extended the scope of his business, adding to the other attractions of his establishment a circulating library, the first of its kind in Scotland. He entered his new shop in May 1726. Sixty years after, the ground-floor of the same *land*, together with the flat where formerly Ramsay was located, were in the occupancy of William Creech, the first of the great Edinburgh Sosii that were yet to include the Constables, the Blackwoods, the Chambers, the Blacks, and others of renown in their day. With the Lucken-booths' premises it is that *The Gentle Shepherd* is always associated. From them Ramsay dated all his editions subsequent to the first two, and there he reaped all the gratifying results of its success.

The poem, which takes its name from the 12th eclogue of Spenser's *Shepherds' Calendar*, whose opening runs as follows—

> 'The Gentle Shepherd satte beside a spring,
> All in the shadow of a bushy brere,'—

may certainly be ranked in the same category with the *Idylls* of Theocritus, Bion, and Moschus, the *Aminta* of Tasso, the *Pastor Fido* (faithful shepherd) of Guarini, and Spenser's great poem referred to above. In *The Gentle Shepherd* Ramsay rises to a level of poetic strength, united to a harmony between conception and execution, so immeasurably superior to anything else he accomplished, that it has furnished matter for speculation to his rivals and his enemies, whether in reality the poem were his own handiwork, or had been merely fathered by him. Lord Hailes, however, pricks this bubble, when dealing with the ill-natured hypothesis raised by Alexander Pennecuik—the doggerel poet, not the doctor—that Sir John Clerk and Sir William Bennet had written *The Gentle Shepherd*, when he remarks, 'that they who attempt to depreciate Ramsay's fame, by insinuating that his friends and patrons composed the works which pass under his name, ought first to prove that his friends and patrons were capable of composing *The Gentle Shepherd.*' Not for a moment can the argument be esteemed to possess logical cogency that, because he never equalled the poem in question in any of his other writings, he was therefore intellectually incapable of composing that masterpiece which will be read after his other productions are forgotten, as long, in fact, as Scots poetry has a niche in the great temple of English literature.

To define pastoral poetry, as Ramsay understood it, without at the same time citing examples lying to hand in the works of our author, is a somewhat difficult task. But as reasons of space will not permit us to duplicate extracts, and as it is proposed to relegate all criticism to the closing chapters of the book, we shall, at present, only glance in passing at the great principles of composition Ramsay kept in view while writing his pastoral.

In the *Guardian*, Addison has stated, with his wonted lucidity and perspicuity, those mechanical rules to which, in his idea, the type of poetry termed 'pastoral' should conform. He maintained it should be a reflection, more or less faithful, of the manners of men 'before they were formed into large societies, cities built, or communities established, where plenty begot pleasure.' In other words, that 'an imaginary Golden Age should be evolved by each poet out of his inner consciousness.' Then the Ursa Major of criticism, Dr. Johnson, after growling at all preceding critics on the subject, and remarking that 'the rustic poems of Theocritus and the eclogues of

Virgil precluded in antiquity all imitation, until the weak productions of Nemesian and Calphurnius, in the Brazen Age of Latin literature,' proceeds to say : 'At the revival of learning in Italy it was soon discovered that a dialogue of imaginary swains might be composed with little difficulty, because the conversation of shepherds excludes profound or refined sentiment.' Rapin, in his *De Carmine Pastorali*, observes : ''Tis hard to give rules for that in which there have been none already given. Yet in this difficulty I will follow Aristotle's example, who, being to lay down rules concerning epics, proposed Homer as a pattern, from whom he deduced the whole art. So will I gather from Theocritus and Virgil, those fathers of pastoral, what I deliver on this account, their practice being rules in itself.' And Pope, in his *Discourse on Pastoral Poetry*, says : 'Since the instructions given for any art are to be delivered as that art is in perfection, they must of necessity be derived from those in whom it is acknowledged so to be. It is therefore from the practice of Theocritus and Virgil (the only undisputed authors of pastoral) that the critics have drawn the foregoing notions concerning it.' And Boileau, in his *Art Poetique*, after cautioning writers of pastoral against the introduction of bombast splendour or pomp on the one hand, and the use of low and mean language on the other, making shepherds converse *comme on parle au village*, observes that 'the path between the two extremes is very difficult'; while Dryden, in his preface to Virgil's *Pastorals*, defines pastoral to be 'the imitation of a shepherd considered under that character.' Finally, to quote Dr. Johnson once more, he remarks, in his *Lives of the Poets*, 'truth and exactness of imitation, to show the beauties without the grossness of country life, should be the aim of pastoral poetry.'

By all these critics pastoral poetry is considered in its abstract or ideal form. They never dreamed of bidding poets descend to the concrete, or to actual rural life, as Beattie puts it, ' there to study that life as they found it.' Dr. Pennecuik justly remarks, in his essay on *Ramsay and Pastoral Poetry* : ' Of the ancient fanciful division of the ages of the world into the *golden*, *silver*, *brazen*, and *iron*, the first, introduced by Saturn into Italy, has been appropriated to the shepherd state. Virgil added this conceit to his polished plagiarisms from Theocritus ; and thus, as he advanced in elegance and majesty, receded from simplicity, nature, reality, and truth.'

To Ramsay's credit be it ascribed, that he broke away from these rank absurdities and false ideas of pastoral poetry, and dared to paint nature and rural life as he found it. His principles are thus stated by himself: ' The Scottish poet must paint his own country's scenes and his own country's life, if he would be true to his office. . . . The morning rises in the poet's description as she does in the Scottish horizon ; we are not carried to Greece and Italy for a shade, a stream, or a breeze ; the groves rise in our own valleys, the rivers flow from our own fountains, and the winds blow upon our own hills.'

To the fact that Ramsay has painted Scotland and Scottish rustics as they are, and has not gone to the hermaphrodite and sexless inhabitants of a mythical Golden Age for the characters of his great drama, the heart of every Scot can bear testimony. Neither Burns, supreme though his genius was over his predecessors, nor Scott, revelling as he did in patriotic sentiments as his dearest possession, can rival Ramsay in the absolute truth wherewith he has painted Scottish rustic life. He is at one and the same time the Teniers and the Claude of Scottish pastoral—the Teniers, in catching with subtle sympathetic insight the precise 'moments' and incidents in the life of his characters most suitable for representation; the Claude, for the almost photographic truth of his reproductions of Scottish scenery.

That Ramsay was influenced by the spirit of his age cannot be denied, but he was sufficiently strong, both intellectually and imaginatively, to yield to that influence only so far as it was helpful to him in the inspiration of his great work, but to resist it when it would have imposed the fetters of an absurd mannerism upon the 'machinery' and the 'atmosphere' of his pastoral. The last decades of the seventeenth, and the first two or three of the eighteenth centuries, were periods when pastoral poetry was in fashion. Italian and French literary modes were supreme. Modern pastoral may be said to have taken its rise in the *Admetus* of Boccaccio; in the introductory act of the *Orfeo* of Politian, written in 1475, and termed *Pastorale*, and in the *Arcadia* of Jacopo Sanazzara. But, according to Dr. Burney, the first complete pastoral drama prepared for the stage was the *Sacrificio Favola Pastorale* of Agostino de Beccari, afterwards published in *Il Parnasso Italiano*. They followed the *Aminta* of Tasso and the *Filli di Sciro* of Bonarelli in the beginning of the seventeenth century. In Italy and France, thereafter, pastoral became the literary mode for the time being; to Clement

Marot, with his *Complaint of Louise of Savoy*, belonging
the honour, as Professor Morley says, of producing the
first French pastoral. It invaded all the fine arts,—music,
painting, sculpture, romance, were all in turn conquered
by it. From France it spread to England and to
Scotland, and thereafter a flood of shepherds and
shepherdesses, of Strephons and Chloes, of Damons,
Phyllises, and Delias, spread over literature, of which the
evidences in England are Spenser's *Shepherds' Calendar*,
Sidney's *Arcadia* ; and in Scotland, Robert Henryson's
Robene and Makyne. Nor did Milton disdain this form
for his *Lycidas*; Pope also affected it, as well as Ambrose
Philips ; while, under the title of *The Shepherd's Week*,
Gay produced one of the most charming of his many
charming works, in which our age, by consigning them
to oblivion, has deliberately deprived itself of genuine
poetic enjoyment. To the extent of the name, and of
that only, was Ramsay influenced by his time. As
regards all else he struck out a new line altogether.

With regard to the *locale* where Ramsay laid the scene
of the drama, two places have laid claim to it ; the first,
and the least probable, being situate near Glencorse,
about seven miles from Edinburgh ; the second, one and
a half miles from the village of Carlops, about twelve
miles distant from the metropolis, and five farther on
from the first - mentioned spot. The balance of probability lies strongly in favour of the Carlops 'scene.' In
the first named, only the waterfall and one or two minor
details can be identified as corresponding to the natural
features of the scenery in the poem ; in the second, every
feature named by Ramsay is full in view. Here are
'the harbour - craig,' 'the trottin' burnie,' 'the little

linn' making 'a singin' din,' 'the twa birks,' 'the pool
breast-deep,' 'the washing-green,' 'the loan,' 'Glaud's
onstead,' 'Symon's house,' 'the craigy bield,' 'Habbie's Howe' or house, and many others.   Another
strong point is that in Act ii. scene 2 of *The Gentle
Shepherd*, Glaud threatens to set his biggest peat-stack
on fire, through sheer joy over Sir William Worthy's
prospective return.   Around the Glencorse site for the
action of the drama, there is not a peat to be dug in the
whole parish ; at the Carlops 'scene,' peat is the staple
fuel of the district.   Near by, also, is Newhall, the
estate which in Ramsay's days was in possession of the
Forbes family, who had purchased it from Dr. Pennecuik,
the author of the *Description of Tweeddale* and other
works.   John Forbes of Newhall was one of Ramsay's
dearest friends, and many relics of the poet are still
preserved at the mansion house ; but it was with the
Pennecuik family Ramsay associated his poem.   In *The
Gentle Shepherd*, Sir William Worthy is described as
having had to fly into exile—

> ' Our brave good master, wha sae wisely fled,
> And left a fair estate to save his head ;
> Because, ye ken fu' weel, he bravely chose
> To stand his liege's friend wi' great Montrose.'

Newhall was purchased by Dr. Pennecuik's father two
years before Charles I. was beheaded.   The doctor
himself was contemporary with Cromwell, Montrose,
Monk, and Charles II., all of whom appear so distinctly
in the pastoral as associated with the action of the piece.
He had to go into hiding during the Commonwealth, for
his support of Charles I., and for sheltering Montrose
after the battle of Philiphaugh.   Pennecuik the younger

(great-grandson of the doctor), in his *Life of Ramsay*, states that the poet appeared to have been indebted to Dr. Pennecuik for the *Story of the Knight*, but to have drawn the character from that of his friend Sir David Forbes.

The issue of the successive editions of *The Gentle Shepherd*, though occupying a large share of his time not engrossed by the cares of business, did not altogether preclude him from writing some fresh pieces when occasion arose. In 1727 appeared a 'Masque,' which was performed at the celebration of the nuptials of James, Duke of Hamilton, and the Lady Ann Cochrane. In this form of poetry Ramsay revived a good old type very popular amongst the Elizabethan poets and dramatists, and even descending down to the days of Milton, whose *Masque of Comus* is the noblest specimen of this kind of composition in modern literature. Ramsay's *dramatis personæ* are rather a motley crew, but on the whole he succeeds in managing the dialogue of his gods, and goddesses very creditably, though any admirer of his genius can see it moves on stilts under such circumstances. *The Pastoral Epithalamium* upon the marriage of George Lord Ramsay and Lady Jean Maule is of a less ambitious cast, both as regards form and thought; the consequence being, that the poet succeeds admirably in expressing the ideas proper to the occasion, when he was not bound by the fetters of an unfamiliar rhythm.

Ramsay's later poems had in turn attained, numerically speaking, to such bulk as fairly entitled him to consider the practicability of issuing a second quarto volume, containing all of value he had written between 1721 and

1728. From all quarters came requests for him so to do. Therefore, towards the close of 1728 he issued his second volume of collected poems. The interest awakened by *The Gentle Shepherd* still burned with a clear and steady glow. From this fact, gratifying, indeed, as regards the proximate success of the individual book, but prophetic also in an ultimate sense of the stability of reputation to be his lot in the republic of letters, he concluded, as he says in one of his letters to the Clerks of Penicuik, 'to regard himself as ane o' the national bards of Scotland.' That he was justified in doing so, the future amply testified.

The realisation that he had now won for himself a permanent place in the literature of his land operated, however, rather injuriously upon the continued fecundity of his genius. He became timorous of further appeals to the public, lest he should injure his fame. Allan Ramsay, in his own eyes, became Ramsay's most dreaded rival. At length he deliberately adopted the resolution that the better part of valour was discretion, and that he would tempt fortune in verse no more. With the exception of his poetical epistle to the Lords of Session, and his volume of metrical *Fables*, Ramsay's poetical career was completed. Henceforth he was occupied in preparing the successive editions of his *Works* and of the *Tea-Table Miscellany*, and in compiling his collection of *Scots Proverbs*.

CHAPTER VIII

RAMSAY had now reached the pinnacle of his fame.
He was forty - four years of age, prosperous in
business, enjoying a reputation not alone confined to
Great Britain, but which had extended to France, to
Holland, and to Italy. His great pastoral was lauded in
terms the most gratifying by critics everywhere as the
most perfect example of the pure idyll that had appeared
since the days of Theocritus. The proudest of the
nobility were not ashamed to take his arm for a walk
down High Street, or to spend an hour cracking jokes
and discussing literature with him under the sign of Ben
Jonson and Drummond of Hawthornden.

What Chambers says in his *Eminent Scotsmen*, from
which are culled the following facts, is strictly accurate :
' Ramsay had now risen to wealth and high respectability, numbering among his familiar friends the best
and the wisest men in the nation. By the greater part
of the Scottish nobility he was caressed, and at the
houses of some of the most distinguished of them,
Hamilton Palace, Loudoun Castle, etc., was a frequent
visitor.' With Duncan Forbes, Lord Advocate (and
before many years to be Lord President), with Sir John

7

Clerk of Penicuik, Sir William Bennet of Marlefield, Sir Alexander Dick of Prestonfield, near Edinburgh, he lived in the habit of daily, familiar, and friendly intercourse. With contemporary poets his relations were likewise of the most friendly kind. The two Hamiltons, of Bangour and Gilbertfield, were his constant associates. To Pope, to Gay, and to Somerville; to Meston, to Mitchell, and to Mallet, he addressed poetical greetings, and several of them returned the salutations in kind. From England, too, came another and a different proof of his popularity, in the fact that, when in 1726 Hogarth published his 'Illustrations of Hudibras' in twelve plates, these were dedicated to 'William Ward of Great Houghton, Northamptonshire, and Allan Ramsay of Edinburgh.' Edinburgh itself was proud of her poet, and was not averse to manifesting the fact when fitting opportunity offered. He was a frequent visitor at the University, and Dugald Stewart relates that an old friend of his father informed him, the students of the fourth and fifth decades of last century used to point out a squat, dapper, keen-eyed little man, who was wont to walk up and down the space in front of their classrooms with Professors Drummond and Maclaurin, as 'the great poet, Allan Ramsay.' The narrator also added, he felt a secret disappointment when thus viewing for the first time a real live poet, and noting that he differed neither in dress nor mien from ordinary men. From his studies among the classics, and from the prints in the early editions of Horace and Virgil, he had been led to imagine the genus poet always perambulated the earth attired in flowing singing robes, their forehead bound with a chaplet, and carrying with them a substantial looking lyre!

The year 1728 had witnessed, as we have seen, the publication of Allan Ramsay's last original work. Thereafter he was content to rest on his laurels, to revise new editions of his various poems, and to add to his *Tea-Table Miscellany* and *Scots Songs*. Perhaps he may have been conscious that the golden glow of youthful imagination at life's meridian, had already given place to those soberer tints that rise athwart the mental horizon, when the Rubicon of the forties has been crossed. In 1737, when writing to his friend Smibert, the painter (then in Boston, America, whither he had emigrated), Ramsay states, with reference to his relinquishment of poetry: 'These six or seven years past I have not written a line of poetry; I e'en gave over in good time, before the coolness of fancy that attends advanced years should make me risk the reputation I had acquired.' He then adds in the letter the following lines of poetry, from which we gather, further, that his determination was the result, not of mere impulse, pique, or chagrin, but of reasoned resolve—

> ' Frae twenty-five to five-and-forty,
> My muse was neither sweer nor dorty ;
> My Pegasus would break his tether,
> E'en at the shaking of a feather,
> And through ideas scour like drift,
> Straking his wings up to the lift.
> Then, then my soul was in a low,
> That gart my numbers safely row ;
> *But eild and judgment 'gin to say,*
> *Let be your sangs and learn to pray.'*

By 1730, then, Ramsay's work, of an original kind at least, was over. In that year, however, he published another short volume of metrical fables, under the title,

A Collection of Thirty Fables. Amongst them we find some of the most delightful of all our poet's work in this vein. *Mercury in Quest of Peace, The Twa Lizards, The Caterpillar and the Ant,* and *The Twa Cats and the Cheese,* possess, as Chalmers truly says, 'all the *naïveté* of Phædrus and La Fontaine, with the wit and ease of Gay.'

And thus Ramsay's literary career closed, after well-nigh two decades of incessant intellectual activity. Begun, as Professor Masson says, 'in the last years of the reign of Queen Anne, and continued through the whole of the reign of George I., it had just touched the beginning of that of George II. when it suddenly ceased. Twice or thrice afterwards, at long intervals, he did scribble a copy of verses ; but in the main, from his forty-fifth year onwards, he rested on his laurels. Henceforward he contented himself with his bookselling, the management of his circulating library, and the superintendence of the numerous editions of his *Collected Poems,* his *Gentle Shepherd,* and his *Tea-Table Miscellany.*'

In pursuance of this determination, Ramsay, in 1731, at the request of a number of London booksellers, edited a complete edition of his works, wherein all the poems published in the quartos of 1721 and 1728 were included, in addition to *The Gentle Shepherd.* The success attending this venture was so great that, in 1733, a Dublin edition had to be prepared, which also handsomely remunerated both author and publishers. From the American colonies, likewise, came accounts of the great popularity of Ramsay's poems, both among the inhabitants of the towns and the settlers in the mighty forests. Of the latter, many were Scotsmen, and to them the vividly realistic scenes and felicitous character-drawing of *The Gentle Shepherd* touched, with a power and a pathos almost overwhelming, the subtlest fibres of that love for 'Caledonia, stern and wild,' which, deepened by distance as it is, and strengthened by absence, seems so inwoven with the very warp and woof of the nature of her children that, go where they will, it can never be eradicated, until the last great consummation overtakes them, when earth returns to earth, ashes to ashes, and dust to dust.

Our poet now had more time on his hands for those social duties and convivial pleasures wherein he took such delight. His new premises in the Luckenbooths, facing down towards, and therefore commanding a full view of, the magnificent thoroughfare of the High Street, were immediately opposite the ancient octagonal-shaped Cross of Edinburgh, where all official proclamations were made. The vicinity of the Cross was, on favourable afternoons, the fashionable rendezvous of the period. No sooner was the midday dinner over, than the fair ladies and gallants of the town—the former in the wide hoops, the jewelled stomachers, the silken *capuchins* (cloaks), the *bongraces* (hoods), and high head-dresses of the day; the latter in the long, embroidered coats, knee-breeches, silk stockings, and buckled shoes, tye-wigs, and three-cornered hats peculiar to the fourth decade of last century—issued from their dingy turnpike stairs in the equally darksome closes, pends, and wynds, to promenade or lounge, as best pleased them, in the open space around the Cross. Here were to be met all sorts and conditions of men and women. Viewed from the first storey of the building wherein Allan Ramsay's shop was situated, the scene must have been an exceed-

ingly animated one. Mr. Robert Chambers, with that
graphic power of literary scene-painting he possessed in
measure so rich, represented the picture, in his *Traditions of Edinburgh*, in colours so vivid, and with a
minuteness of detail so striking, that subsequent descrip-
tions have been little more than reproductions of his.
Let us take advantage of his admirable sketch of the
scene round the Cross, filling in any important details
he may have omitted.

The jostlement and huddlement was extreme everywhere. Ladies and gentlemen paraded along in the
stately attire of the period : grave Lords of Session, and
leading legal luminaries, bustling Writers to the Signet
and their attendant clerks, were all there. Tradesmen
chatted in groups, often bareheaded, at their shop doors ;
caddies whisked about, bearing messages or attending to
the affairs of strangers ; children darted about in noisy
sport ; corduroyed carters from Gilmerton are bawling
'coals' and 'yellow sand'; fishwives are crying their
'caller haddies' from Newhaven ; whimsicals and
idiots going about, each with his or her crowd of tor-
mentors ; *tronmen* with their bags of soot ; town-guards-
men in rusty uniform, and with their ancient Lochaber
axes; water-carriers with their dripping barrels ; Highland drovers in philabeg, sporran, and cap ; Liddesdale
farmers with their blue Lowland bonnets ; sedan chair-
men, with here and there a red uniform from the
castle—such was the scene upon which, in the early
months of the year 1732,—alas ! his last on earth,—the
celebrated London poet, John Gay, gazed from the
windows of Allan Ramsay's shop. Beside him stood
the redoubtable Allan himself, pointing out to him the

most notable personages in the motley crowd, and every
now and then called upon to explain some Scotticism in
his speech which reminded Gay of passages in *The
Gentle Shepherd* that Pope had desired him to get
explained from the author himself. And worthy Allan is
flattered yet flustered withal with the honour, for beside
them stand the famous Duchess of Queensberry—better
known as Prior's 'Kitty,' otherwise Lady Catherine
Hyde, daughter of the Earl of Clarendon—and her
miser husband, who only opened his close fist to build
such palatial piles as Queensberry House, in the Edinburgh Canongate, and Drumlanrig Castle, Dumfries-
shire. They have brought Gay up north with them,
after his disappointment in getting his play—*Polly*, the
continuation of the *Beggars' Opera*—refused sanction for
representation by the Duke of Grafton, then Lord
Chamberlain. Ah! how honest Allan smirks and
smiles, and becks and bows, with a backbone that will
never be as supple in *kotowing* to anyone else. For
does he not, like many more of us, dearly love a lord,
and imagine the sun to rise and set in the mere enjoyment of the ducal smile?

A pleasant visit was that paid by Gay to Scotland in
1732, before he returned to London to die, in the
December of the same year. He spent many of his
spare hours in the company of Ramsay, and that of the
two friends in whose society much of the latter's time was
now to be passed—Sir John Clerk of Penicuik and Sir
Alexander Dick of Prestonfield. By all three, Gay was
deeply regretted,—by Clerk and Dick chiefly, because he
had so much that was akin to their own genial friend,
Allan Ramsay.

In 1736 our poet published a collection of *Scots Proverbs*, which, for some reason or another, has never been printed with his poems in those editions that are professedly complete. Only in Oliver's pocket edition is this excellent thesaurus of pithy and forcible Scottish apophthegms presented with his other works. That it is one of the best repertories of our proverbial current coin that exists, particularly with regard to the crystallised shrewdness and keen observation embodied in them, must be apparent to any reader, even the most cursory. To supersede the trashy works of Fergusson and Kelly was the reason why Ramsay set himself to gather up the wealth of aphoristic wisdom that lay manna-like on all sides of him. As might be expected, it is richest in the sayings common throughout the three Lothians, though the Lowlands, as a whole, are well represented. Of Gaelic proverbs there is scarce a trace, showing how faintly, despite his Jacobitism, his sympathies were aroused by Celtic tradition or Celtic poetry. Many of the sayings were undoubtedly coined in Ramsay's own literary mint, though the ideas may have been common property among the people of his day. But how close the union between the ideas and their expression in this collection! Of looseness of phrase there is scarce a trace. How apt the stereotyping of current idioms in such pithy verbal nuggets as—'Ne'er tell your fae when your foot sleeps,' 'Nature passes nurture,' 'Muckledom is nae virtue,' 'Happy the wife that's married to a motherless son,' 'Farmers' faugh gar lairds laugh.'

Ramsay's dedication of his volume of *Scots Proverbs* to 'The Tenantry of Scotland, Farmers of the Dales and

Storemasters of the Hills,' shows the value he attached
to this kind of literature. He writes in the colloquial
Scots, and his words are valuable as presenting us with
a reliable example of the Scots vernacular as spoken in
educated circles early last century. 'The following
hoard of *Wise Sayings* and observations of our forefathers,' he remarks, 'which have been gathering through
many bygone ages, I have collected with great care, and
restored to their proper sense, which had been frequently
tint [lost] by publishers that did not understand our
landwart [inland] language. . . . As naething helps our
happiness mair than to hae the mind made up with right
principles, I desire you, for the thriving and pleasure of
you and yours, to use your een and lend your lugs to
these guid auld says, that shine wi' wailed sense and will
as lang as the warld wags. Gar your bairns get them by
heart; let them hae a place among your family-books;
and may never a window-sole through the country be
without them. On a spare hour, when the day is clear,
behind a rick, or on the green howm, draw the treasure
frae your pooch and enjoy the pleasant companion. Ye
happy herds, while your hirdsels are feeding on the
flowery braes, ye may eithly mak yoursels masters of the
holy ware.'

Hitherto the sky of Ramsay's life had been well-nigh
cloudless. Misfortune and failure had never shrivelled
his hopes or his enterprises with the frost of disappointment. Nothing more serious than an envious scribbler's
splenetic effusions had ever assailed him. Now he was
to know the sting of mortification and the pinch of
financial loss.

We have already adverted to the gloomy bigotry of a

certain section of the Scottish clergy of this period. To
them everything that savoured of jollity and amusement
was specially inspired by the Evil One, for the hindrance
of their ministerial labours. The references to this matter
are manifold throughout Ramsay's poetry. Though no
one had a deeper respect for vital piety than he, no one
more bitterly reprobated that puritanic fanaticism that
saw sin and wrong - doing in innocent recreation and
relaxation. Against Ramsay the ecclesiastical thunder
had commenced to roll some years before (according to
Wodrow), when he started his circulating library. That
the works of Shakespeare, Beaumout and Fletcher, Ben
Jonson, Massinger, Dryden, Waller, and the romances of
chivalry, should be placed in the hands of the youth of
Edinburgh, was accounted a sin so grave as to merit
Presbyterial censure. Accordingly, a party, amongst
whom was the infamous Lord Grange, attempted to
suppress the library. But the *ægis* of the redoubtable
Dr. Webster had been thrown over him, and the pother
in time died away. It appears, however, that Ramsay, in
1736, had imported a large stock of translations of the
most celebrated French plays of the day, and had added
them to his library. Sufficient was this to blow into
a blaze the smouldering embers of clerical indignation.
From pulpit and press our poet was fulminated at. Not
that he gave the smallest sign that he cared one jot for
all their denunciations. He attended to his shop and
his library, and quaffed his claret at the *Isle of Man Arms*,
at Luckie Dunbar's in Forrester's Wynd, or at the famous
John's Coffee House, with the cynical response that 'they
might e'en gang their ain gate.'

But just at this precise time Ramsay conceived the

idea of becoming a theatre-proprietor, and thus benefit-
ing the worthy burgesses of Auld Reekie by erecting a
house where standard dramas might be performed. The
very proposal raised a storm of indignation in clerical
circles, against which even Dr. Webster and his friends
were powerless. Hitherto the opposition of the Presbyterian ministers had prevented the erection of any theatre
in the town. The companies of itinerating players who
might chance to visit the town from time to time, were
compelled to hire a hall or a booth for their perform-
ances. Prior to the Commonwealth, *histrionic* exhibitions
were frequent in Edinburgh. But from 1650 to the
Union, fanaticism became paramount and sternly re-
pressed them. One of the earliest mentions of dramatic
representations after that date occurs in 1710, and again
in 1715, when a regular company of players performed
certain dramas in the Long Gallery and in the Tennis
Court at Holyrood-house. In the subsequent winter, as
we learn from the *Scots Courant* of December 16, 1715,
the plays were represented in the old magazine-house at
the back of the foot of the Canongate, on which occasion,
said the notice, 'the several parts would be performed
by some new actors just arrived from England.'

On the last night of the year 1719 Ramsay supplied
a prologue for the performance of Otway's play, 'The
Orphan,' and 'The Cheats' of Scapin, 'by some young
gentlemen,' wherein he remarked—

'Somebody says to some folk, we're to blame;
That 'tis a scandal and a burning shame
To thole young callants thus to grow sae snack,
And learn—O mighty crimes!—to speak and act!
But let them talk. In spite of ilk endeavour,
We'll cherish wit, and scorn their fead or favour.'

In 1722 he wrote an epilogue, to be spoken after the acting of 'The Drummer'; in 1726 a prologue, to be addressed to the audience by the famous Tony Aston on the first night of his appearance; in 1727 a prologue, to be delivered before the acting of 'Aurenzebe,' at Haddington School; and finally, an epilogue, recited after the performance of 'The Orphan' and 'The Gentle Shepherd,' in January 1729. All these, and probably others that have not been preserved, evince that Ramsay cherished a warm affection for the drama, with an earnest desire to see his fellow-countrymen profit by it. After the indignant remonstrance—

> ' Shall London have its houses twa,
> And we be doomed to nane ava?
> Is our metropolis ance the place
> Where lang-syne dwelt the royal race
> Of Fergus, this gait dwindled doun
> To the level o' a *clachan* toun?
> While thus she suffers the desertion
> Of a maist rational diversion,'

he commenced to erect, in 1736, a playhouse in Carrubber's Close. In his advertisement in the *Caledonian Mercury*, announcing the prospective opening, he states, he had built the house 'at vast expense,' in order that, during the winter nights, the citizens might enjoy themselves in hearing, performed by competent actors, dramas that would amuse, instruct, and elevate.

His advertisement, in the issue of the *Mercury* for September 15, 1736, reads:—

' The new theatre in Carrubber's Close being in great forward-ness, will be opened on the 1st of November. These are to advertise the ladies and gentlemen who incline to purchase annual tickets, to enter their names before the 20th of October next, on which day they shall receive their tickets from Allan Ramsay, on paying 30s., no more than forty to be subscribed for ; after which none will be disposed of under two guineas.'

Meantime the clerical party and the enemies of Ramsay had joined hands in common opposition to his plans. 'Hardly had he begun operations' (writes Professor Masson) 'when there came the extraordinary statute of 10 Geo. II. (1737), regulating theatres for the future all over Great Britain. As by this statute, there could be no performance of stage plays out of London and Westminster, save when the king chanced to be residing in some other town, Ramsay's speculation collapsed.' In fact, the municipal authorities, at the instigation of the clergy, employed the force of the statute peremptorily to close his theatre. In vain he appealed to law. 'He only received a quibble for his pains. He was injured without being damaged,' said the lawyers. In vain he appealed in a poetical epistle, to President Duncan Forbes of the Court of Session, wherein he says—

> ' Is there aught better than the stage
> To mend the follies o' the age,
> If managed as it ought to be,
> Frae ilka vice and blaidry free?
> Wherefore, my Lords, I humbly pray
> Our lads may be allowed to play,
> At least till new-house debts be paid off,
> The cause that I'm the maist afraid of ;
> Which lade lyes on my single back,
> And I maun pay it ilka plack.'

Well might the good-hearted, honourable-minded poet dread the future. The responsibility lay upon him alone for the expense of the building, and from many intima-

tions he let drop the failure of the speculation well-nigh
ruined him. But the increasing sale of his books, and
the expanding prosperity of his business, soon recouped
his outlay. That he was much depressed by his losses,
heavy and unexpected as they were, is evident from a
private letter he wrote at this time to the President, and
which is still preserved at Culloden House. 'Will you,'
he writes, 'give me something to do? Here I pass a
sort of half-idle, scrimp life, tending a trifling trade that
scarce affords me the needful. Had I not got a parcel
of guineas from you, and such as you, who were pleased
to patronise my subscriptions, I should not have had a
gray groat. I think shame—but why should I, when I
open my mind to one of your goodness?—to hint that I
want to have some small commission, when it happens
to fall in your way to put me into it.'

Not without an element of pathos is the scene that is
here presented, of him, who had done so much to amuse
and elevate his fellows, being compelled to make such a
request. Satisfactory is it, however, to know that, though
the poetical epistle 'to the Lords' was fruitless of
practical benefit in the way he desired, albeit exciting
for him the warmest sympathy among the worthy
senators of the College of Justice, there is reason to
believe the President was able to throw 'some small
commission' in Ramsay's way, and thus, by his opportune
generosity, to dispel the thunderclouds of misfortune
hurrying hard upon the poet's steps.

Of course, to his enemies (amongst whom was Pennecuik, the poet), as well as to the more bigoted of the
clergy, his trials were a judgment upon his conduct. A
shoal of pamphlets and pasquinades appeared, as though

to rub salt into the raw wounds of his mortified feelings :
such despicable effusions—written in more than one case
by 'ministers of the Gospel'—as 'The Flight of Religious
Piety from Scotland, upon account of Ramsay's lewd
books and the Hell-bred comedians, who debauch all
the Faculties of the Soul of our Rising Generation,' ' A
Looking-Glass for Allan Ramsay,' 'The Dying Words
of Allan Ramsay,' etc. As Chalmers remarks : 'The
lampooners left intimations of what must have been of
considerable consolation to our adventurous dramatist;
that "he had acquired wealth"; that "he possessed a
fine house"; that "he had raised his kin to high degree."'
Such topics of censure did more honour than hurt to
Ramsay. To their ribald raillery the poet replied only
by a contemptuous silence, infinitely more galling than if
he had turned on the wasps and crushed them, thus be-
speaking for them a prominence in no measure merited.
Their spleen he forgot amid the engrossments of a closer
attention to business, and the charms of friendship's
intercourse.

It may be added, however, that the whirligig of time
brought in for Ramsay his revenges upon his enemies.
The theatre which in 1746 was erected in Playhouse
Close in the Canongate, though only by a quibbling
evasion of the statute, so Draconic were its provisions,
was largely due to his energy and exertions. Thus, says
a biographer, Ramsay, at the age of sixty, had the
satisfaction to see dramatical entertainments enjoyed
by the citizens, whose theatrical tastes he had kindled
and fostered.

CHAPTER IX

LITTLE more of a biographical character is there to relate. The last seventeen years of Ramsay's life were passed in the bosom of his family, and in attention to his business. His son, Allan—afterwards an artist of great celebrity, and portait painter to George III.,—after studying, as the proud father informs his friend Smibert in a letter about this time, with Mr. Hyffidg in London, and spending a little time at home 'painting like a Raphael,' had been sent to Rome, where he made good use of his opportunities. The father's heart yearns over the boy, and he pathetically adds : 'I'm sweer to part with him, but canna stem the current which flows from the advice of his patrons and his own inclination.' His three daughters were growing up into 'fine, handsome girls,' while 'my dear auld wife is still my bedfellow.'

What a beautiful picture we get of the kindly old poet, drawn unconsciously by himself in this letter. Domesticity and parental affection were two qualities pre-eminently present in Ramsay's nature.

From Mrs. Murray of Henderland we also receive a delicious side-peep into Allan's character. In 1825 she

informed Mr. Robert Chambers that ' he was one of the
most amiable men she had ever known. His constant
cheerfulness and lively conversational powers had made
him a favourite amongst persons of rank, whose guest
he frequently was. Being very fond of children, he
encouraged his daughters in bringing troops of young
ladies about the house, in whose sports he would mix
with a patience and vivacity wonderful in an old man.
He used to give these young friends a kind of ball once
a year. From pure kindness for the young, he would
help to make dolls for them, and cradles wherein to
place these little effigies, with his own hands.'

From 1740 to 1743 he enjoyed to the full the idyllic
happiness and peace described in his epistle to James
Clerk of Penicuik—

> ' Though born to not ae inch of ground,
> I keep my conscience white and sound ;
> And though I ne'er was a rich heaper,
> To make that up I live the cheaper ;
> By this ae knack I've made a shift
> To drive ambitious care adrift ;
> And now in years and sense grown auld,
> In ease I like my limbs to fauld.
> Debts I abhor, and plan to be
> Frae shochling trade and danger free,
> That I may, loos'd frae care and strife,
> With calmness view the edge of life ;
> And when a full ripe age shall crave,
> Slide easily into my grave.'

In 1742, finding himself in a position to take more
ease than his busy life had hitherto permitted to him, he
bought a piece of ground on the Castlehill, overlooking
the valley of the North Loch, and there erected that
curious house, with its octagonal-shaped frontage, copied

8

from a Neapolitan villa, and designed by his son Allan, which so long was an ornament on the northern slope overlooking the New Town of Edinburgh. From his windows a reach of scenery was commanded, probably not surpassed in Europe, stretching from the mouth of the Firth of Forth on the east to the Grampians on the west, and extending far across the green hills of Fife to the north. The poet, however, becoming alarmed at the expense he was incurring, altered his son's design after the building was half completed. In consequence, the mansion presented a very quaint appearance. Tradition states that Andrew Fletcher of Saltoun (afterwards Lord Milton) first detected the resemblance to a goose-pie. Be this as it may, Allan was grievously vexed by the comparison, and one day, when showing it, in the pride of his heart, to the witty Lord Elibank, who duly admired its unrivalled prospect, he added, 'And yet, my lord, thae toon wits say it's like naething else than a guse-pie.' 'Deed, Allan, noo I see ye intilt, I'm thinkin' the wits are no' sae far wrang.' History does not record Allan's rejoinder.

Scarcely had he entered his new mansion, however, expecting to enjoy there many years of domestic happiness and peace, than the great sorrow of his life fell upon him. In March 1743, his faithful and loving partner, who had stood by him amid all the storm and stress of his busy career, was taken from him, after thirty years of unbroken affection and devotion. She was interred in the Greyfriars Churchyard, as the cemetery records show, on the 28th of March 1743. So intense was her husband's grief that he, who for many another had written elegies instinct with deep sympathy and regret, could not trust himself to write of her, 'lest I should break doon a'thegither into my second bairn-hood.' Alas! poor Allan!

But his daughters, realising to the full the part that now devolved on them, stepped into the gap left in his domestic circle. Nobly they fulfilled their duty, and amongst the most affecting tributes Ramsay paid, is that to the filial affection of 'his girls,' over whom, after their mother had gone from them, he watched with a wealth of paternal love and an anxious solicitude, as unsparing as it was unremitting.

And thus did the life of Allan Ramsay roll quietly onward through placid reaches of domestic and social happiness, during the closing fourteen years of existence. Though he did not formally retire from business until 1755, he left it almost entirely in the hands of capable subordinates. He had worked hard in his day, and now, as he said—

> ——' I the best and fairest please,
> A little man that lo'es my ease,
> And never thole these passions lang
> That rudely mint to do me wrang.'

Accordingly, he lived quietly in the 'goose-pie,' 'fauld-ing his limbs in ease,' and absolutely refusing to concern himself with anything political, social, or ecclesiastical calculated to bring worry and trouble upon him.

During the Rebellion of 1745, tradition states that Prince Charles Edward, after the capture of the city by the Highland army, sent a message to Ramsay, asking him to repair to Holyrood, that some mark of his new sovereign's favour might be bestowed on him. Singular, indeed, it was, that the poet should have selected the day in question to repair to his friend James Clerk's mansion at Penicuik, and that he should there have been seized with so severe an indisposition as to prevent him returning to Edinburgh for nearly five weeks. Though a Tory and a Jacobite, honest Allan knew upon which side his bread was buttered. Such honours as would have been conferred would have been inconvenient. Moreover, the Rebellion had not yet attained dimensions sufficient to transmute it from a rebellion into a revolution. Pawkiness and caution were prominent traits in his character, and they were never used to more salient advantage than in the instance in question.

To the end of life, Ramsay remained the same kindly, genial, honourable man, whose appearance in any of the social circles he frequented, was the signal for 'quips and cranks and wreathèd smiles' to go round, and for the feast of reason and the flow of soul to commence. His squat, podgy figure waddling down the High Street on his way to his shop in the Luckenbooths, his head covered with the quaint three-cornered hat of the period, beneath which peeped his tie-wig, was one of the familiar sights of Edinburgh, to be pointed out to strangers with a pride and an affection that never diminished. In his little villa on the Castlehill he entertained his friends in true Horatian style, and with a hospitality every whit as warm, though it was every whit as simple as that which the great Roman promised Mæcenas, he made them free of what was in his power to give.

Foibles he had,—and who is without them? faults, too, —for what character lacks them? yet his very foibles and his faults leaned to virtue's side. Vain he certainly was, deny the fact who can? his egotism, also, may have jarred on some whose individuality was as strong as his own, but whose liberality in making allowances for human weaknesses was less. Nay, he may even in some respects have been 'near' with regard to certain little things, though this was the result of his humble upbringing, where, in the household economy of the Crichtons, a pound was a fortune. But once break through the crust of his old-fashioned formalism with the thrust of some pressing appeal for aid, and instantly we touch the core of a ready and warm sympathy—a sympathy as catholic in the radius of its beneficence as it was munificent in the measure of its benefactions. To the poor, to the suffering, to the widow and the orphan, to the fatherless and the friendless, Allan Ramsay was ever the readiest to help where help was really needed; and if his vanity liked the fact to be made public property, wherein lay the harm? Do our published subscription-lists to-day not testify to the existence of the same foible in nine-tenths of us? To the improvident, however, to the lazy, to the genteel beggar, and to the thousand and one forms mendicity—supported by mendacity—takes to extort money, Allan was as adamant. 'Gang your wa's,' he would say to such; 'gar your elbuck earn what your mooth eats, and ye'll be a better man.'

Allan has had the misfortune to be rated by what he did not do in the way of charity, rather than by what he did. Because he esteemed charity to begin at home, and that he should provide for his own before partici-pating in any schemes for providing for others, he has been rated as selfish and miserly. The opposite is the case. Prudent, careful, and economical,—into no speculation would he go from which he did not see the probability, at least, of an adequate return. Hence, during the South Sea madness, he kept his head when many a better man went mad with the speculative mania. He was pious, without his piety being black-edged with that gloomy bigotry which characterised much of the Presbyterianism of the seventeeenth and eighteenth centuries in Scotland. As he put the matter himself in his *Epistle to James Arbuckle :*

> ' Neist, Anti-Toland, Blunt, and Whiston,
> Know positively I'm a Christian,
> Believing truths and thinking free,
> Wishing thrawn parties would agree.'

He delighted in sociality and conviviality, but recoiled from aught savouring of licence or excess. To coarseness, it is true, he may at times have stooped in his work ; but we must remember the spirit of the times was in favour of calling a spade a spade, and not 'an implement for disintegrating planetary particles.' To no degree greater than did Swift, or Steele, or Arbuthnot, or Gay, can Allan Ramsay be considered to have smirched his pages with references either ribald or indelicate. The spirit of the age was in fault when coarseness was rated as wit; and to be true to life, the painters of the manners around them had to represent these as they were, not as they would have liked them to be.

On the 9th May 1755 Ramsay, when writing to his friend, James Clerk of Penicuik, a rhyming epistle, had said—

> ' Now seventy years are o'er my head,
> And thirty mae may lay me dead.'

Alas ! the 'Shadow feared of man' was already sitting waiting for him at no great distance farther on in his life's journey. For some years he had suffered acutely from scurvy in the gums, which in the end attacked his jawbone and affected his speech. To the close, however, he retained his cheerfulness and buoyancy of spirits. When the last great summons at length came to him, he met it with a manly fortitude and Christian resignation.

Amongst his last words, according to his daughter Janet, who survived until 1807, were these: 'I'm no' feared of death; the Bricht and Morning Star has risen and is shining mair and mair unto the perfect day.' And so he passed 'into the unseen' on the 7th January 1758, in the seventy-second year of his age. He was interred two days after in the Greyfriars Churchyard, where his gravestone is still visible, bearing the inscription: 'In this cemetery was interred the mortal part of an immortal poet, Allan Ramsay, author of *The Gentle Shepherd* and other admirable poems in the Scottish dialect. He was born in 1686 and died in 1758.

> 'No sculptured marble here, no pompous lay,
> No storièd urn, no animated bust;
> This simple stone directs pale Scotia's way
> To pour her sorrows o'er her poet's dust.[1]
>
> Though here you're buried, worthy Allan,
> We'll ne'er forget you, canty callan;
> For while your soul lives in the sky,
> Your " Gentle Shepherd " ne'er shall die.'

Sir John Clerk, one of the Barons of the Exchequer in Scotland, who admired his genius and was one of his most intimate friends, erected at his family seat at Penicuik an obelisk to his memory; while Mr. Alexander

[1] The first stanza is in reality by Burns, and is identical with that he placed on the tombstone he erected over the remains of Fergusson, the poet, in the Canongate Churchyard.

Fraser-Tytler, at Woodhouselee, near the Glencorse *locale* of *The Gentle Shepherd*, has erected a rustic temple which bears the inscription—

'ALLANO RAMSAY ET GENIO LOCI.

'Here midst those streams that taught thy Doric Muse
Her sweetest song,—the hills, the woods, and stream,
Where beauteous Peggy strayed, list'ning the while
Her Gentle Shepherd's tender tale of love.
Scenes which thy pencil, true to Nature, gave
To live for ever.   Sacred be this shrine;
And unprofaned, by ruder hands, the stone
That owes its honours to thy deathless name.'

Ramsay was survived by his son Allan, the painter, and by his two daughters, Christian and Janet, who amongst them inherited the poet's fortune.   The house on the Castlehill fell to his son, and remained in the possession of the family, as Mr. Logie Robertson records, until 1845, when it changed hands at the death of General John Ramsay, the poet's grandson, and the last of his line.   For many years it stood, an object of interest to all admirers of the bard, until 1892, when, just as the building was beginning to show signs of age, the site was bought for the erection of the new students' boarding-house, 'University Hall,' which so imposingly crowns the ridge of the Castlehill.   With a reverence for the memory of the poet as rare as it is commendable, the promoters of the scheme resolved to preserve as much as possible of the house, and the greater part of it has been incorporated in the new building.

Of Ramsay we have only two portraits remaining that are of any real value,—that painted by his son Allan, and that by Smibert, the poet's lifelong friend.   The latter represents him in youth, the former in age—both being considered, at the time of execution, striking likenesses. But perhaps the best idea of the appearance of the poet may be gathered from Sir John Steele's fine statue of him (designed from his son's portrait) which now stands at the corner of West Princes Street Gardens, Edinburgh, immediately below the site of his house.   There, with his familiar 'nightcap' on his head, he stands, watching the busy crowds passing to and fro in front of him, wearing the while an expression on his face as though he were saying with his Patie—

> ' He that hath just enough can soundly sleep,
> The o'ercome only fashes fouk to keep ;
> Content's the greatest bliss we can procure
> Frae 'boon the lift : without it, kings are poor.'

CHAPTER X

RAMSAY AS A PASTORAL POET AND AN ELEGIST

In attempting a critical estimate of the value of Ramsay's works, for the purpose of analysis it will be most convenient to consider the great body of his writings under certain classified headings—(1) Ramsay as a Pastoral Poet and an Elegist; (2) Ramsay as a Satirist and a Song-writer; (3) Ramsay's Miscellaneous Works.

In the chapter on *The Gentle Shepherd*, we noted the distinctive constituents of pastoral poetry, as currently defined, and also wherein Ramsay's principles, as exemplified in practice, differ from those of other writers of pastoral. To furnish examples illustrative of our contention is now all that remains to be done. Early in his poetical career, as soon, in fact, as he had completed his first tentative efforts, Ramsay seems to have become conscious, with that rare gift of prevision always distinguishing him, that his strength lay in a picturesque yet truthful delineation of rural life. His earliest pieces, although termed elegies, exhibit, rather, many of the characteristics of pastorals, in the broad humour and in the graphic and vivid colouring wherewith he depicts the scenes at Maggy Johnston's tavern at Morningside, or the incidents in the life of Luckie

Wood or of Patie Birnie. But, as he has termed them
elegies, under that heading let them be considered,
though a humorous or mock elegy is somewhat of a
contradiction in terms.

Roughly classified, Ramsay's pastorals may be stated
as follows:—the dialogues between *Richy* (Sir Rich.
Steele) *and Sandy* (Alex. Pope), on the death of Mr.
Addison; between *Robert, Richy, and Sandy,* on the
death of Matthew Prior; *Keitha,* on the death of the
Countess of Wigton; an *Ode with* a *Pastoral Recitative,*
on the marriage of James Earl of Wemyss to Miss Janet
Charteris; *A Masque,* performed at the celebration of
the nuptials of James Duke of Hamilton and Lady Ann
Cochrane; *A Pastoral Epithalamium,* on the marriage
of George Lord Ramsay and Lady Jean Maule; *Betty
and Kate,* a pastoral farewell to Mr. Aikman; and finally,
The Gentle Shepherd.

Of Ramsay's less important pastorals, the distinguishing characteristics are their simplicity, their tenderness,
and their freedom from aught didactic. In conforming
to the conventional idea of pastoral,—the idea, that is,
of the shepherd state being a condition of perfect peace
and Arcadian felicity and propriety,—in place of copying
direct from nature, they one and all differ from *The
Gentle Shepherd.* The picture of burly Sir Richard
Steele and of crooked little Alexander Pope, clad in
shepherd's weeds, and masquerading with dogs and
pipes and what not, savours somewhat of the ludicrous.
Then, in *Richy and Sandy,* he makes Pope bewail the
death of Addison, with whom he had been on anything
but friendly terms for years previous; while the following
picture of the deceased grave-visaged Secretary of State,

in such a position as described in the following lines, tends to induce us profane Philistines of these latter days, to smile, if not to sneer—

> ' A better lad ne'er leaned out o'er a kent,
> Nor hounded collie o'er the mossy bent :
> Blythe at the bughts how oft hae we three been,
> Heartsome on hills, and gay upon the green.'

This, however, was the fashion in vogue, and to it our poet had to conform. In *Richy and Sandy*, in *Robert, Richy, and Sandy*, and in his earlier pastorals generally, we seem to see the poet struggling to rid himself of the conventional prejudices against painting rural nature in the real, and in favour of 'a golden-age rusticity' purely imaginary. Not by this is it implied that I claim for our poet the credit of first insisting on reverting to nature for the study of scenes and character. The same conviction, according to Lowell, was entertained by Spenser, and his *Shepherds' Calendar* was a manifestation, however imperfect and unsatisfactory, of his desire to hark back to nature for inspiration. In *Keitha* the same incongruity, as noted above, is visible. The poem in question, with that on the *Marriage of the Earl of Wemyss*, can neither be ranked as conventional pastoral nor as pure pastoral, according to Ramsay's later style. We note the 'Colins' and 'Ringans,' the 'shepherd's reeds' and 'shepherd's weeds,' and the picture of

> ——' the singing shepherd on the green
> Armyas hight, wha used wi' tunefu' lay
> To please the ear when he began to play,'

—an imitation of Milton's immortal lines in *Comus*, which are too well known to need quotation. All of a piece this with the 'golden-age pastoral.' In the same

poems, however, occur intimations that the incongruity
was perceived by the author, but that, as yet, he did not
see any means of remedying the uniform monotony
of the conventional form. The leaven was at work
in Ramsay's mind, but so far it only succeeded in
influencing but the smallest moiety of the lump.

In the *Masque*, written in celebration of the marriage
of the Duke of Hamilton, the sentiments expressed are
wholly different. Written subsequently to *The Gentle
Shepherd*, Ramsay exhibited in it his increased technical
deftness, and how much he had profitted by the experience gained in producing his great pastoral. The
Masque, albeit professedly a dramatic pastoral, entirely
abjures the lackadaisical shepherds and shepherdesses of
conventional pastoral, and, as a poem of pure imagination,
reverts to the ancient mythology for the *dramatis personæ*.

All these pieces, however, though they exhibit a facility
in composition, a fecundity of imagination, a skilful
adaptation of theme to specific metrical form, a rare
human sympathy, and a depth of pathos as natural in
expression as it was genuine in its essence, are only, so
to speak, the preludes to *The Gentle Shepherd*. In the
latter, Ramsay's matured principles of pastoral composition are to be viewed where best their relative importance
can be estimated, namely, when put into practice.

By competent critics, *The Gentle Shepherd* is generally
conceded to be the noblest pastoral in the English
language. Dr. Hugh Blair, in his lectures on *Rhetoric
and Belles Lettres*, styled it ' a pastoral drama which will
bear being brought into comparison with any composition
of this kind in any language. . . . It is full of so much
natural description and tender sentiment as would do

honour to any poet. The characters are well drawn, the incidents affecting, the scenery and manners lively and just.' And one of Dr. Blair's successors in the Chair of Rhetoric and English Literature in the University of Edinburgh,—a man and a Scotsman who, in his day, has done more than any other to foster amongst our youth a love of all that is great and good and beautiful in our literature; a teacher, too, whose students, whom he has imbued with his own noble spirit, are scattered over the world, from China to Peru,—Emeritus-Professor David Masson, has observed in his charming *Edinburgh Sketches*: 'The poem was received with enthusiastic admiration. There had been nothing like it before in Scottish literature, or in any other: nothing so good of any kind that could be voted even similar; and this was at once the critical verdict.'

To anyone who will carefully compare the *Idylls* of Theocritus, the *Eclogues* of Virgil, and the *Aminta* of Tasso, with Ramsay's great poem, the conviction will be driven home,—in the face, it may be, of many deeply-rooted prejudices,—that the same inspiration which, like a fiery rivulet, runs through the three former master-pieces, is present also in the latter — that inspiration being the perfect and unbroken homogeneity existing between the local atmosphere of the poem and the characteristics of the *dramatis personæ*. This fact it is which renders the *Aminta* so imperishable a memorial of Tasso's genus; for it is Italian pastoral, redolent of the air, and smacking of the very soil of sunny Italy. The symmetrical perfection of *The Gentle Shepherd*, in like manner, is due to the fact that the feelings and desires and impulses of the characters in the pastoral are those distinctively native and proper to persons in their sphere of life. There is no dissidence visible between what may imperfectly be termed the *motif* of the poem and the sentiments of even the most subordinate characters in it. Therein lies the true essence of literary symmetry —the symmetry not alone of mere form, though that also was present, but the symmetry resulting from the harmony of thought with its expression, of scene and its characters, of situation and its incidents. Such the symmetry exhibited by Homer's *Iliad*, by Dante's *Inferno*, by Milton's *Paradise Lost*, by Cervantes' *Don Quixote*, by Camoens' *Lusiad*, by Scott's *Lay of the Last Minstrel*, by Tennyson's *Idylls*.

Frankly, it must be admitted that only in his *Gentle Shepherd* does Ramsay attain this outstanding excellence. His other pieces are meritorious,—highly so; but they could have been produced by many a writer of the age with equal, perhaps superior, felicity, and they shine only in the reflected light of *The Gentle Shepherd*; even as Scott's *Lord of the Isles* and *Harold the Dauntless* were saved from being 'damned as mediocrity' only by the excellence of the *Lay of the Last Minstrel* and *Marmion*.

The great charm of *The Gentle Shepherd* lies in the skilfully-balanced antithesis of its contrasts, in the reflected interest each type casts on its opposite. As in Molière's *Tartuffe*, it is the vivid contrast created between the hypocrisy of the title-character and the easy good-nature of Orgon, that begets a reciprocal interest in the fortunes of both; as in Balzac's *Père Goriot*, it is the pitiless selfishness of his three daughters on the one hand, and the doting self-denial of the poor old father on the other, that throws both sets of characters into relief so strong: so, in *The Gentle Shepherd*, it is the subtle force of the contrast between Patie's well-balanced manliness and justifiable pride, and Roger's *gauche* bashfulness and depression in the face of Jenny's coldness; between Peggy's piquant lovableness and maidenly joy in the knowledge of Patie's love, and Jenny's affected dislike to the opposite sex to conceal the real state of her feelings towards Roger in particular, that impart to the poem the vivid interest wherewith its scenes are perused. Minor contrasts are present too, in the faithfulness of Patie to Peggy, as compared with the faithlessness of Bauldy to Neps. The whole drama, in fact, might be styled a beautiful panegyric on fidelity in love. Such passages as the following are frequent—

> ' I'd hate my rising fortune, should it move
> The fair foundation of our faithfu' love.
> If at my feet were crowns and sceptres laid
> To bribe my soul frae thee, delightful maid,
> For thee I'd soon leave these inferior things
> To sic as have the patience to be kings.'

As a pastoral poet, Ramsay excels in painting all those homely virtues that befit the station to which most of his characters belonged. A fault, and a serious one, it was among the writers of conventional pastoral, to make their shepherds and shepherdesses talk like philosophers, and reason upon all the mysteries of life, death, and futurity. What reader of Sir Philip Sidney's *Arcadia*, but must have smiled over the shepherds in that delicious romance discussing love, and treating of its metaphysical causes and effects, as profoundly as any

> —— ' clerke of Oxenforde also
> Who unto logik hadde long y-go.'

The extravagances of conventional pastoral had been keenly satirised by Gay, who made his Lobbin Clouts and Cloddipoles, his Blowzalinds and Bowzabees and Bumkinets, in the *Shepherd's Week*, 'talk the language that is spoken neither by country maiden nor courtly dame; nay, not only such as in the present time is not uttered, but never was in times past, and, if I judge aright, will never be uttered in times future.' But by Ramsay the silliness of the prevailing mode, both of British and French pastoral, was more aptly satirised, by presenting, as a contrast, a picture of rural life absolutely truthful in all its details, and thus slaying falsehood by the sword of truth.

Of *The Gentle Shepherd*, the plot is simplicity itself. It describes the love of a young Pentland shepherd named Patie for a country maiden named Peggy. The pastoral drama, the time of whose action is all embraced within four-and-twenty hours, thus preserving one, at least, of the Greek dramatic unities as defined by the French critics, opens at early morning with the two young shepherds, Patie and Roger, feeding their flocks on the hills, and discussing the progress of their love-suits. The scene is charmingly realistic and natural. Patie is happy in his love for Peggy who reciprocates it; Roger, in despair over his ill-success with 'dorty Jenny.' His friend, however, raises his spirits by telling him how he once served Peggy when she had a fit of tantrums, by feigning indifference to her, a course which soon brought the fair one to reason. He exhorts Roger to adopt the same line, conveying his counsel in the following terms, that contain excellent advice to young lovers,

9

and might have given a hint to Burns for his song,
'Duncan Gray'—

> 'Dear Roger, when your jo puts on her gloom,
> Do ye sae too, and never fash your thumb;
> Seem to forsake her, soon she'll change her mood;
> Gae woo anither, and she'll gang clean wood.'

Roger agrees to take the advice, and the scene concludes
with a delightful picture of a shepherd's meal—

> 'But first we'll tak a turn up to the height,
> And see gif all our flocks be feeding right;
> By that time, bannocks and a shave of cheese
> Will make a breakfast that a laird might please,—
> Might please the daintiest gabs, were they sae wise
> To season meat with health instead of spice.
> When we have ta'en the grace-drink at this well,
> I'll whistle syne'—

The second scene opens with an exquisite description of

> 'A flowrie howm between twa verdant braes,
> Where lasses use to wash and spread their claes;
> A trottin' burnie wimpling through the ground,
> Its channel, pebbles, shining, smooth and round.
> Here view twa barefoot beauties, clean and clear.'

These are Peggy and Jenny. The latter proposes to
begin their work on the 'howm' or green in question,
but Peggy entreats her to

> 'Gae farer up the burn to Habbie's How,
> Where a' that's sweet in spring and simmer grow;
> Between twa birks out o'er a little linn
> The water fa's, and makes a singin' din;
> A pool breast-deep, beneath as clear as glass,
> Kisses wi' easy whirles the bordering grass.
> We'll end our washing while the morning's cool,
> And when the day grows het we'll to the pool,
> There wash oursels; 'tis healthfu' now in May,
> And sweetly cauler on sae warm a day.'

The girls then enter on a discussion regarding Jenny's cruel indifference to Roger. The maiden, who by the way is a bit of a prude, affects to despise love and marriage, but in the end, overcome by Peggy's beautiful description of conjugal happiness, is obliged to confess her love for Roger. What more delightful picture of maternal yearning over the young have we in all English literature, than Peggy's splendid defence of motherhood?—

> 'Yes, it's a heartsome thing to be a wife,
> When round the ingle-edge young sprouts are rife.
> Gif I'm sae happy, I shall have delight
> To hear their little plaints, and keep them right.
> Wow, Jenny! can there greater pleasure be,
> Than see sic wee tots toolying at your knee;
> When a' they ettle at,—their greatest wish,
> Is to be made of and obtain a kiss?
> Can there be toil in tenting day and night
> The like of them, when love makes care delight?'

The first scene of the Second Act opens with a picture of a peasant farmer's 'onstead'; to wit, his dwelling and outhouses—

> 'A snug thack-house; before the door a green;
> Hens on the midden, ducks in dubs are seen;
> On this side stands a barn, on that a byre:
> A peat stack joins, and forms a rural square.'

Here the neighbours, Glaud and Symon, meet. The latter has been into Edinburgh to sell his 'crummock and her bassened quey,' and over their pipes he informs his friend that their landlord, Sir William Worthy, who, as a Royalist, had been compelled to go into exile during the Commonwealth, would now, owing to the Restoration, be able to return home again, when all would be well. Symon has heard the news from the laird's servant,

'Habbie,' after whom the 'How' or *house* is named.
Glaud is so overjoyed at the news that he seeks to
persuade Symon to remain and dine with him, offering,
for it was before the age of good roads and carts,

> 'To yoke my sled, and send to the neist town
> And bring a draught o' ale baith stout and brown.'

But Symon wishes to exercise hospitality himself, and
insists upon Glaud, his sister Madge, his daughter Jenny,
and his niece Peggy, all dining with him, in honour of
the day. This they are to do. We have here presented
a graphic picture of rural fare on fête-days—

> 'For here yestreen I brewed a bow of maut,
> Yestreen I slew twa wethers prime and fat.
> A furlet of good cakes, my Elspa beuk,
> And a large ham hangs reesting in the neuk.
> I saw mysel', or I cam o'er the loan,
> Our muckle pot that scads the whey, put on,
> A mutton-bouk to boil, and ane we'll roast;
> And on the haggies Elspa spares nae cost.
> Small are they shorn, and she can mix fu' nice
> The gusty ingans wi' a curn of spice;
> Fat are the puddings,—heads and feet weel sung.'

The second scene introduces a new element into the
drama. Another shepherd, Bauldy (Archibald) by name,
has also been smitten with Peggy's charms—and it affords
an excellent idea of the simplicity of these rural districts
in Scotland, when he repairs to a poor old woman
named Mause, whom the district reputes to be a witch,
to entreat her aid in turning Peggy's heart towards
himself. Bauldy's picture of Peggy, in his soliloquy, is
beautiful in its very simplicity—

> 'O Peggy! sweeter than the dawning day,
> Sweeter than gowany glens or new-mawn hay;

Blyther than lambs that frisk out o'er the knowes,
Straighter than aught that in the forest grows.
Her een the clearest blob of dew out-shines,
The lily in her breast its beauty tines ;
Her legs, her arms, her cheeks, her mouth, her een,
Will be my deid '—

The existence of superstition among the Scottish peasantry, a state of things lasting until well on into last century, is also well brought out in Bauldy's soliloquy, when he refers to Mausy, 'a witch that for sma' price, can cast her cantrips, and gie me advice.' Mause, meaning to read the faithless lover of Neps a lesson, consents to help him. The fourth scene of the Second Act is undoubtedly one of the finest in the drama—the meeting of the lovers, Patie and Peggy. The two great constituents of a successful piece, strength and pathos, are both present in rich measure. To test her lover's fidelity, the maiden, with coy coquetry, affects to think that he might alter his mind and deceive her if she trusted him too implicitly. To this Patie replies that she deeply wrongs him in doubting his fidelity, and that he would be dull and blind

' Gif I could fancy aught's sae sweet and fair
As my sweet Meg, or worthy of my care.
Thy breath is sweeter than the sweetest brier,
Thy cheek and breast the finest flowers appear,
Thy words excel the maist delightfu' notes
That warble through the merle or mavis' throats ;
With thee I tent nae flowers that busk the field,
Or ripest berries that our mountains yield ;
The sweetest fruits that hing upon the tree
Are far inferior to a kiss frae thee.'

With all a loving woman's sweet perversity, however, Peggy still affects to doubt, only to be indulged in the delicious bliss of hearing her lover's vows anew—

> 'Sooner a mother shall her fondness drap,
> And wrang the bairn sits smiling in her lap ;
> The sun shall change, the moon to change shall cease ;
> The gaits to climb, the sheep to yield the fleece ;
> Ere aught by me be either said or done
> Shall do thee wrang ;—I swear by all aboon.'

In no scene does Ramsay exhibit his wonderful knowledge of the human heart to such advantage as in the one before us. Peggy and Patie then sing a duet, taking alternate verses, into which are introduced many of the old Scots songs,—'The Broom o' Cowdenknowes,' 'Milking the Ewes,' 'Jenny Nettles,' 'Thro' the Wood, Laddie,' 'The Boatman,' 'Maggie Lauder,' 'The Lass o' Patie's Mill,' and the curtain falls over one of the most delightful scenes illustrative of pure affection, in modern drama.

The Third Act sees the return of Sir William Worthy, who, in the disguise of a wizard, introduces himself into the company, merry-making at Symon's. Here he tells Patie's fortune, and the surprising discovery is ere long made that the youth is Sir William's only son, placed under Symon's care when the knight had to go into exile on the execution of Charles I. The description of the little festivity at Symon's is well wrought out. The third scene contains the love-making of Jenny and Roger, where the faithful swain's happiness is rendered complete. With great gusto Ramsay paints this episode, as well as with consummate fidelity to nature,—a fact becoming increasingly apparent when one notes the marked difference between the love-scene wherein

Patie and Peggy take part, and that wherein Jenny declares her love for Roger. The latter scene is more decidedly tinged with rusticity than the former. In the fourth scene Sir William reveals himself to Symon, and inquires eagerly about the progress made by his son during his years of absence. Symon praises the youth's devotion to letters, and then hints at his love for Peggy, which Sir William declares must be forgotten.

The first scene of the Fourth Act relieves, by the introduction of humorous episodes, the sentimentality whereinto the drama at this stage shows signs of lapsing. Mause, Madge, and Bauldy have an interview, at which the two last named come to blows; and when Bauldy has taken himself off, the two women perfect their plans for playing on the foolish fellow's superstitious fears. The remainder of the Fourth Act deals with Patie's sorrow and Peggy's anguish when Sir William's decision is made known. Of course, they vow everlasting fidelity to each other. The scene between the lovers is a very powerful one, wherein Ramsay evinced his sway over the subtler emotions. Yet here, as elsewhere, his simplicity constitutes his strength. He never attempts to depict any complex interaction of human passions. Like Æschylus, he contents himself with the representation of one elemental emotion at a time, and he thoroughly exhausts the one ' *moment* ' before he passes on to another. Few passages are there in literature more genuinely pathetic, yet keeping more rigidly within the modesty of nature, than that wherein poor Peggy, after dwelling on the golden past, tries to picture the dull grey round of duty in the future when Patie shall have been taken from her—

> 'Speak on, speak ever thus, and still my grief;
> But short, I dare to hope the fond relief.
> New thoughts a gentler face will soon inspire,
> That with nice airs swims round in silk attire;
> Then I, poor me! with sighs may ban my fate,
> When the young laird's nae mair my heartsome Pate.
> Nae mair again to hear sweet tales expresst
> By the blyth shepherd that excelled the rest,—
> Nae mair be envied by the tattling gang
> When Patie kissed me when I danced or sang;
> Nae mair, alake! we'll on the meadows play,
> And rin half-breathless round the rucks of hay,
> As aft-times I have fled from thee right fain,
> And fa'n on purpose, that I might be tane.'—

But Patie reiterates his vows to her, and Peggy, comforted, declares she will set herself to learn 'gentler charms, through ilka school where I may manners learn.' Patie applauds her resolution, but declares that

> ——'without a' the little helps of art
> Thy native sweets might gain a prince's heart,
> Yet now, lest in our station we offend,
> We must learn modes to innocence unken'd.'

The scene closes with Peggy's vows of fidelity. In this scene Ramsay touched the high-water mark of his genius, and for the elements of simplicity, strength, and propriety of the sentiments expressed by each character with the root-idea of that character, it is rivalled by very few scenes of its kind in the literature of our land.

The first scene of the last Act opens with Bauldy's fright. He had gone to fulfil his engagement to meet Mause, the pretended witch, who was to turn Peggy's heart to him. But as he had insulted Madge, Peggy's aunt, in the fore part of the day, the latter, to punish him by taking advantage of his dread of ghosts, meets him at the dead hour of the night when he is repairing to Mause's cottage. She is draped in a white sheet, and utters ghastly groans. Bauldy, having sunk terror-stricken to the ground, is soundly cuffed and trounced by the two women. As soon, therefore, as daylight breaks, he seeks an interview with Sir William to entreat redress. The latter, who had been passing the night in Symon's house, enters fully into the spirit of the joke, and orders Mause to be brought before him.

The second scene exhibits Glaud's 'onstead' again, and the family preparing to go down to Symon's to take their leave of Patie. Peggy is very sad,—so much so that her sharp-tongued aunt cannot refrain from jeering at it—

> ' Poor Meg !—Look, Jenny, was the like e'er seen ?
> How bleared and red wi' greetin' look her een !
> This day her brankan wooer taks his horse
> To strut a gentle spark at Edinburgh Cross.
> But Meg, poor Meg ! maun wi' the shepherds stay,
> And tak what God will send in hodden gray.'

To this ill-timed speech Peggy makes a pathetic reply, that must have caused a pang of remorse to her aunt. But when Glaud ventures to warn her against being too free with Patie, seeing he could not marry her now, she replies with gentle reproach—

> ' Sir William's virtuous, and of gentle blood ;
> And may not Patrick too, like him, be good?'

Glaud's answer exhibits the simple faith of the rural inhabitants of the district in a striking light—

> ' That's true and mony gentry mae than he,
> As they are wiser, better are than we ;

> But thinner sawn : they're sae pufft up wi' pride,
> There's mony o' them mocks ilk haly guide
> That shows the gate to heav'n. I've heard mysel
> Some of them laugh at doomsday, sin, and hell.'

The last scene of the pastoral contains the *dénouement*. With great artistic skill, so as to avoid wearying the reader, Ramsay only represents the delivering of the verdict upon Bauldy's appeal against Mause, the result being that the former was informed he only got what he deserved. At this moment, however, Madge, Peggy, and Jenny enter the room where Sir William was sitting. On Peggy Sir Williams gazes with interest, but presently starts with surprise. Her features are those of his long-dead sister. Eagerly he inquires from Glaud if she be his daughter. Glaud, after some hesitation, declares her to be a foundling. At this juncture, however, old Mause steps forward and unravels the tangled skein. She first calls on Sir William to say if he does not recall her features as his own old nurse. Sir William joyfully recognises her, and then she relates how she had brought Peggy as a babe thither, to save its life from those who had usurped its rights after his sister's death. She declares that Peggy is indeed his own niece, and Patie's full cousin.

Patie's joy is now complete, and the two lovers, their prospective union blessed by Sir William, fall into one another's arms ; while the happiness of the shepherds and rustics is consummated when Sir William, restored to his possessions, announces his intention never more to leave them. To Symon and Glaud he assigns their *mailings* (farms) in perpetual feu, while Roger is made his chamberlain. As the curtain then descends over general happiness, Sir William pronounces the usual moral admonition, without which no pastoral of the time was complete—

> ' My friends, I'm satisfied you'll all behave,
> Each in his station as I'd wish and crave.
> Be ever virtuous, soon or late ye'll find
> Reward and satisfaction to your mind.
> The maze of life sometimes looks dark and wild,
> And oft when hopes are highest we're beguiled ;
> Oft when we stand on brinks of dark despair
> Some happy turn with joy dispels our care.'

The relative proportions of the various characters have been preserved with rare skill, and the individuality of each is as firmly and clearly differentiated in a few rapid incisive strokes, as though he had expended pages of description on each, like Pope and Gay. Patie's cheery *bonhomie* and vivacious nature, his love of learning and his wise views of life and its duties, find an excellent foil in the slow, bashful, phlegmatic Roger, whose very 'blateness' denies him the bliss he covets in Jenny's love. Peggy is altogether charming,—a lovely, pure-souled, healthful, sport-loving maiden, with enough of her sex's foibles in her to leave her a very woman, yet with as few faults as it is possible for faulty human nature to be without. One of the most delightful heroines in pastoral poetry is Peggy. Jenny's prudish airs and affected dislike to the sterner sex are delicately yet incisively portrayed, while the staunch fidelity of Symon, the cheery chirpiness of Glaud, the bucolic ignorance and superstition of Bauldy, the cankered impatience of Madge—a spinster against her will, and the pathetic, age-worn weariness of Mause, are depicted with the assured hand of a master. Many of the lyrics interspersed throughout the pastoral are gems of rustic song; not high-class poetry, otherwise they would have been as out of place as would the Johnsonian minnows, talking, as Goldsmith said, like whales.

Only to one other production of Ramsay's genius will attention be called under this head, namely, his continuation of James the First's poem, *Christ's Kirk on the Green*. Of this, the first canto only was written by its royal author. Ramsay, therefore, conceived the design of completing it, as was remarked before. The king had painted with great spirit the squabble that arose at a rustic wedding at Christ's Kirk, in the parish of Kinnethmont, in that part of the county of Aberdeen near Leslie called the Garioch. Ramsay seems to have mistaken it for Leslie in Fife. Two cantos were added by our poet to the piece, in the one of which he exhibited the company, their differences ended, as engaging in feasting and good cheer; in the other, their appearance the following morning, after they had slept off the effects of the orgies, and when they proceed to the bridegroom's house to offer gifts. The skill wherewith Ramsay dovetailed his work into that of his royal predecessor, and developed the king's characters along lines fully in accord with their inception, is very remarkable. There is a Rabelaisian element in the headlong fun and broad rough-and-tumble humour Ramsay introduces into his portion of the poem, but it is not discordant with the king's ideas. The whole piece is almost photographic in the vividness of the several portraits; the 'moment' of delineation selected for each being that best calculated to afford a clue to the type of character. The following picture of the 'reader,' or church pre-

centor in Roman Catholic times, has often been admired,
as almost Chaucerian, for its force and truth—

> ' The latter-gae of haly rhime,
>   Sat up at the boord head,
> And a' he said 'twas thought a crime
>   To contradict indeed.
> For in clerk lear he was right prime,
>   And could baith write and read,
> And drank sae firm till ne'er a styme
>   He could keek on a bead
>   Or book that day.'

The coarseness of the pieces cannot be denied. Still,
withal, there is a robust, manly strength in the ideas
and a picturesque force in the vocabulary that covers
a multitude of sins. His picture of morning has often
been compared with that of Butler in *Hudibras*, but
the advantage undoubtedly lies with Ramsay. Butler
describes the dawn as follows—

> ' The sun had long since in the lap
> Of Thetis taken out his nap,
> And, like a lobster boil'd, the morn
> From black to red began to turn.'

Ramsay, in his description, says—

> ' Now frae th' east neuk o' Fife the dawn
>   Speel'd westlines up the lift ;
> Carles wha heard the cock had crawn,
>   Begoud to rax and rift ;
> And greedy wives, wi' girning thrawn,
>   Cry'd "Lasses, up to thrift" ;
> Dogs barkèd, and the lads frae hand
>   Bang'd to their breeks like drift,
>   Be break o' day.'

It must be remembered, the poem was addressed to
rustics, who would neither have understood nor
appreciated anything of a higher or less broadly

Hogarthian nature. In *Christ's Kirk on the Green* we have stereotyped to all time a picture of manners unsurpassed for vigour and accuracy of detail, to which antiquarians have gone, and will go, for information that is furnished in no other quarter.

In his elegies pure and simple, namely, those divested of any humorous element, Ramsay has done good work; but it is not by any means on a par with what is expected from the poet who could write *The Gentle Shepherd*. A painter of low life in its aspects both humorous and farcical was Ramsay's distinctive *métier*. Pity it was his vanity and ambition ever induced him to turn aside from the path wherein he was supreme. His 'Ode to the Memory of Lady Mary Anstruther,' that to 'the Memory of Lady Garlies,' the one to Sir John Clerk on the death of his son James Clerk, and the 'Ode to the Memory of Mrs. Forbes of Newhall,' are his best elegies. The versification is correct, the ideas expressed are sympathetically tender, poetic propriety and the modesty of nature are not infringed by any exaggerated expressions of grief, but the glow of genius is lacking, and the subtle union of sentiment and expression that are so prominent features in his greater poem.

His two finest efforts as an elegist were his *Ode to the Memory of Mrs. Forbes*, beginning—

> ' Ah, life! thou short uncertain blaze,
>   Scarce worthy to be wished or loved,
> Why by strict death so many ways,
>   So soon, the sweetest are removed!
>
> If outward charms and temper sweet,
>   The cheerful smile, the thought sublime,
> Could have preserved, she ne'er had met
>   A change till death had sunk with time;'

also the one on the *Death of Sir Isaac Newton*, wherein
occur two memorable stanzas—

> ' Great Newton's dead !—full ripe his fame ;
> Cease vulgar grief, to cloud our song :
> We thank the Author of our frame,
> Who lent him to the earth so long.
>
> For none with greater strength of soul
> Could rise to more divine a height,
> Or range the orbs from pole to pole,
> And more improve the human sight.'

His 'humorous elegies,' written in a mock heroic
strain, and sometimes upon persons still living, though,
for the purposes of his art, he represented them as dead,
as in the case of John Cowper, are instinct with broad,
rollicking, Rabelaisian fun. Their vivid portrayal of
the manners and customs of the time renders them
invaluable. What better description of the convivial
habits of Edinburgh society early last century could be
desired, than the graphic pictures in *Luckie Wood's Elegy*,
particularly the stanza—

> ' To the sma' hours we aft sat still,
> Nick'd round our toasts and sneeshin'-mill ;
> Good cakes we wanted ne'er at will,
> The best of bread ;
> Which aften cost us mony a gill
> To Aitkenhead.'

Than his elegies on Luckie Spence, John Cowper, and
Patie Birnie, no more realistic presentation of low-life
manners could be desired. They are pictures such as
Hogarth would have revelled in, and to which he alone
could have done justice in reproduction.

CHAPTER XI

RAMSAY AS A SATIRIST AND A SONG-WRITER

DIFFICULT it is to make any exact classification of Ramsay's works, inasmuch as he frequently applied class-names to poems to which they were utterly inapplicable. Thus many of his elegies and epistles were really satires, while more than one of those poems he styled satires were rather of an epic character than anything else. By the reader, therefore, certain shortcomings in classification must be overlooked, as Ramsay's poetical terminology (if the phrase be permissible) was far from being exact.

As I have previously remarked, Ramsay's studies in poetry, in addition to the earlier Scottish verse, had lain largely in the later Elizabethan, Jacobean, and Caroline periods. In these, Milton, Cowley, Dryden, and Pope were his favourites, and their influence is to be traced throughout his satires. To Boileau he had paid some attention, though his acquaintance with French literature was more through the medium of translations, than by drawing directly from the fountainhead. Ramsay's satires exhibit all the virtues of correct mediocrity. Their versification is smooth, and they generally scan accurately: the ideas are expressed pithily, at times epigrammatically and wittily. The faults and foibles satirised in most cases are those that richly merited the satiric lash. Yet, all these merits granted, the reader feels something to be lacking. The reason is not far to seek. Ramsay never felt at home in what may be termed 'polished satire.' He was as much out of place as would a low comedian on being suddenly called upon to undertake 'drawing-room comedy.' Perpetually would he feel the inclination to rap out one of the rousing, though vulgar, jokes that inevitably evoked a roar of applause from the gallery, and sooner or later he would give way to it. Ramsay was in precisely the same position. The consequence is that in the *Morning Interview*, professedly an imitation of Pope's *Rape of the Lock*, there are incongruous images introduced, for the purpose of relieving the piece by humorous comparisons, which offend the taste even of the most cursory reader. Such allusions as that to 'soft fifteen on her feet-washing night,' and others of a cognate character, are entirely out of place in 'polished satire.' If he attempted the type of composition, he ought to have conformed to its rules.

Of course, Ramsay wrote certain satires, *The Last Speech of a Wretched Miser* and the like, in the Scots vernacular, and addressed to the lower classes in the community, where his genius is seen at its best, because dealing with 'low-life satire' and the types of character he loved most of all to paint. But his *Wealth or the Woody*, his *Health*—a poem addressed to Lord Stair, his *Scribblers Lashed*, *The General Mistake*, *The Epistle to Lord Ramsay*, and the *Rise and Fall of Stocks in* 1720, exhibit Ramsay's genius moving in fetters. His touch lacks piquancy and epigrammatic incisiveness,—lacks, too,

10

that determinate deftness so characteristic of Horace,
as well as those subtle *nuances* of double-meaning
wherein Pope and Arbuthnot excelled, and of which the
latter's terrible 'Epitaph on Colonel Chartres' is a
favourable example.   Ramsay hits with the hammer of
Thor, when he should tap as lightly as 'twere reproof
administered by a fair one with her fan.   Witness his
portrait of Talpo in *Health*—a poem in many respects
one of Ramsay's best.   With what airy satiric touches
Pope or Gay would have dashed off the character.
Note the laboured strokes wherewith Ramsay produces
his picture—

> 'But Talpo sighs with matrimonial cares,
>   His cheeks wear wrinkles, silver grow his hairs,
>   Before old age his health decays apace,
>   And very rarely smiles clear up his face.
>   Talpo's a fool, there's hardly help for that,
>   He scarcely knows himself what he'd be at.
>   He's avaricious to the last degree,
>   And thinks his wife and children make too free
>   With his dear idol; this creates his pain,
>   And breeds convulsions in his narrow brain.
>   He's always startled at approaching fate,
>   And often jealous of his virtuous mate;
>   Is ever anxious, shuns his friends to save:
>   Thus soon he'll fret himself into a grave;
>   There let him rot'—

But Ramsay's distinguishing and saving characteristic
in satire was the breadth and felicity of his humour.
To satire, however, humour is less adapted than wit,
and of wit Ramsay had, in a comparative sense, but a
scanty endowment.   He was not one of those who
could say smart things, though he could depict a
humorous episode or situation as felicitously as anyone

of his age. Like Rabelais, he was a humorist, not a wit, and his satires suffered accordingly. Perhaps the best of his satires is *The Last Speech of a Wretched Miser*, wherein his humour becomes bitingly sardonic. The wretch's address to his pelf is very powerful—

> 'O dool! and am I forced to dee,
> And nae mair my dear siller see,
> That glanced sae sweetly in my e'e!
>   It breaks my heart!
> My gold! my bonds! alackanie
>   That we should part.

> Like Tantalus, I lang have stood,
> Chin-deep into a siller flood;
> Yet ne'er was able for my blood,
>   But pain and strife,
> To ware ae drap on claiths or food,
>   To cherish life.'

Different, indeed, is the case when we come to consider Ramsay as a song-writer and a lyrist. To him the former title rather than the latter is best applicable. This is not the place to note the resemblances and the differences between the French *chanson*, the German *lied*, the Italian *canzóne*, and the English song or lyric. But as indicating a distinction between the two last terms, Mr. F. T. Palgrave, in the introduction to his invaluable *Golden Treasury of Songs and Lyrics*, regards a 'lyric' as a poem turning on 'some single thought, feeling, or situation'; Mr. H. M. Posnett, in his thoughtful volume on *Comparative Literature*, remarks that the lyric has varied from sacred or magical hymns and odes of priest bards, only fulfilling their purpose when sung, and perhaps never consigned to writing at all, down to written expressions of individual feeling from which all accompaniments of dance or music have been severed. But approximately defined, a lyric may be said to be a poem—short, vivid, and expressive of a definite emotion, appealing more to the eye than with any ultimate view of being set to music; a song, as a composition appealing more to the ear, wherein the sentiments are more leisurely expressed, with the intention of being accompanied by music. Mr. E. H. Stoddard, in the preface to his *English Madrigals*, defines a lyric 'as a simple, unstudied expression of thought, sentiment, or passion; a song, its expression according to the mode of the day.' The essence of a lyric is point, grace, and symmetry; of a song, fluency, freedom, and the expression of sympathetic emotions.

Ramsay, according to this basis of distinction, was, as has been said, rather a song-writer than a lyrist. The works of Shakespeare, Ben Jonson, Beaumont and Fletcher, and Massinger, abound in lyrics, but contain comparatively few songs, in the modern sense of the word, in which we speak of the songs of Burns, Moore, and Barry Cornwall. Ramsay, in his songs, sacrificed everything to mode. In nine cases out of ten he had the tune for the song in his mind when he was writing the words. In Scotland, as is well known, there is an immense body of music, some of it ancient, some of it comparatively modern, though none of it much later than the Restoration. That was the mine wherein Ramsay dug long and deep for the music for his *Tea-Table Miscellany*. To those ancient tunes he supplied words—words that to this day remain as a memorial of the skill and sympathy wherewith he wedded the spirit of the melodies to language in keeping with their national character.

To a *soupçon* of diffuseness the poet must, however, plead guilty—guilty, moreover, because of the invincible temptation to pad out a line now and then 'for crambo's sake' when the ideas ran short. Ramsay possessed all the qualities constituting a song-writer of great and varied genius. His work exhibits ease and elasticity of rhythm, liquid smoothness of assonance, sympathetic beauty of thought, with subtle skill in wedding sense to sound. Though his verse lacked the dainty finish of Herrick and Waller, the brilliant facet-like sparkle of Carew, Suckling, and Lovelace, the tender grace of Sedley, and the half-cynical, half-regretful, but wholly piquant epicureanism, of Rochester and Denham, yet Ramsay had a charm all his own. Witness the 'Lass o' Patie's Mill'; is it not entirely *sui generis*?

> 'The lass o' Patie's Mill,
>   So bonny, blythe, and gay,
> In spite of all my skill,
>   She stole my heart away.
> When tedding of the hay,
>   Bareheaded on the green,
> Love midst her locks did play,
>   And wantoned in her een.
>
> Her arms, white, round, and smooth,
>   Breasts rising in their dawn,
> To age it would give youth
>   To press 'em with his hand.
> Thro' all my spirits ran
>   An ecstasy of bliss
> When I such sweetness fan'
>   Wrapt in a balmy kiss.
>
> Without the help of art,
>   Like flowers that grace the wild,
> She did her sweets impart
>   Whene'er she spoke or smil'd.

> Her looks they were so mild,
>   Free from affected pride,
> She me to love beguiled,
>   I wished her for my bride.'

Take also 'Bessy Bell and Mary Gray'; what a rich fancy and charming humour plays throughout the piece, united to a keen knowledge of the human heart—

> 'O Bessy Bell and Mary Gray,
>   They are twa bonny lasses;
> They bigg'd a bower on yon burnbrae,
>   And theek'd it o'er with rashes.
> Fair Bessy Bell I loo'd yestreen,
>   And thought I ne'er could alter;
> But Mary Gray's twa pawky e'en,
>   They gar my fancy falter,'

or that verse in his 'Scots Cantata,' with what simplicity, yet with what true pathos, is it not charged?—

> 'O bonny lassie, since 'tis sae,
>   That I'm despised by thee,
> I hate to live; but O, I'm wae,
>   And unco sweer to dee.
> Dear Jeany, think what dowy hours
>   I thole by your disdain:
> Why should a breast sae saft as yours
>   Contain a heart of stane?'

George Withers' famous lines, 'Shall I, wasting in despaire,' are not a whit more pathetic. Then if we desire humour pure and unadulterated, where can be found a more delightful *lilt* than 'The Widow'?

> 'The widow can bake, and the widow can brew,
>   The widow can shape, and the widow can sew,[1]
> And mony braw things the widow can do,—
>   Then have at the widow, my laddie.'

---

[1] Pronounced in Scots, *shoo.*

Or if you affect a dash of satire in your songs, what more to your taste than—

> 'Gi'e me a lass wi' a lump o' land,
>   And we for life shall gang thegither,
> Though daft or wise I'll ne'er demand,
>   Or black or fair it maks na whether.
> I'm aff wi' wit, and beauty will fade,
>   And blood alane is no worth a shilling;
> But she that's rich, her market's made,
>   For ilka charm aboot her's killing.'

Or if the reader desire the wells of his deepest sympathies to be stirred, what more truly pathetic than his 'Auld Lang Syne,' which supplied Burns with many of the ideas for his immortal song; or his version of 'Lochaber No More'—

> 'Farewell to Lochaber, and farewell my Jean,
> Where heartsome wi' thee I've mony day been;
> For Lochaber no more, Lochaber no more,
> We'll maybe return to Lochaber no more,'

—a song than which to this day few are more popular among Scotsmen. As a song-writer Ramsay appeals to all natures and all temperaments. He was almost entirely free from the vice of poetic conventionality. He wrote what seemed to him best, undeterred by the dread of offending against poetic canons, or the principles of this, that, or the other school of poetry. He was a natural singer, not one formed by art—a singer, voicing his patriotic enthusiasm in many a lay, that for warmth of national feeling, for intense love of his species, for passionate expression of the tenderer emotions, is little behind the best of the songs of Robert Burns. Granted that his was not the power to sweep, like Burns, or Béranger, or Heine, with masterful hand over the entire gamut of human passions; that to him was not given, as to them, the supremely keen insight into the workings of the human heart, and the magical witchery of wedding sense to sound so indissolubly, that alter but a word in the texture of the lines and the poem is ruined. Yet, in his province, Ramsay was dowered with a gift but little less notable, that of portraying so faithfully the natural beauties of his country, and the special characteristics of his country-men, that, in a greater degree even than Burns,— were Ramsay's songs only recognised as his, in place of being ascribed to others,—he has a right to the proud title of Scotland's national song-writer. Not for a moment do I seek to place Ramsay on a pedestal co-equal with Burns — that were an error worse than folly; not for a moment do I seek to detract from the transcendent merit of our great national poet. But though I do not rate Burns the less, I value Ramsay the more, when I say that, had there been no Ramsay there might have been no Burns nor any Fergusson — at least, the genius of the two last named poets would not have found an adequate vehicle of expression lying readymade to their hand. Ramsay it was who virtually rendered the Scots vernacular a possible medium for the use of Burns; and this service, unconsciously rendered by the lesser genius to the greater, is generously acknowledged by the latter, who could not but be aware that, as his own star waxed higher and yet higher from the horizon line of popularity, that of his elder rival waned more and more. Therefore his

noble panegyric on Ramsay is but a tribute to his
'father in song'—

> 'Thou paints auld nature to the nines,
> In thy sweet Caledonian lines;
> Nae gowden stream through myrtle twines,
>   Where Philomel,
> While nightly breezes sweep the vines,
>   Her griefs will tell.
>
> In gowany glens thy burnie strays,
> Where bonnie lassies bleach their claes;
> Or trots by hazelly shaws and braes,
>   Wi' hawthorns gray,
> Where blackbirds join the shepherd's lays
>   At close o' day.
>
> Thy rural loves are nature's sel';
> Nae bombast spates o' nonsense swell;
> Nae snap conceits, but that sweet spell
>   O' witchin' love,
> That charm that can the strongest quell,
>   The sternest move.'

CHAPTER XII

RAMSAY'S MISCELLANEOUS POEMS; CONCLUSION

OUR survey is now drawing to a close. To say a word upon those miscellaneous poems that do not fall naturally into any convenient category for classification is all that remains to be done.

Already attention has been called to the poem on *Content*, when its purpose was sketched. Though containing many passages of no little power and beauty, yet as a whole it is heavy and uninteresting. Written during the time when the glamour of Pope's influence was upon Ramsay, it exhibits many of Pope's faults without his redeeming features. True, the characters are drawn with great vigour and distinctive individuality, but the trail of dulness lies over it, and *Content* slumbers, with James Thomson's *chef d'œuvre* on *Liberty*, on the top shelf amongst the spiders. The description of the palace of the goddess Content has, however, often been praised for its vigorous scene-painting—

> ' Amidst the glade the sacred palace stood,
> The architecture not so fine as good;
> Nor scrimp, nor gousty, regular and plain,
> Plain were the columns which the roof sustain;
> An easy greatness in the whole was found,
> Where all that nature wanted did abound:

But here no beds are screen'd with rich brocade,
Nor fuel logs in silver grates are laid;
Nor broken China bowls disturb the joy
Of waiting handmaid, or the running boy;
Nor in the cupboard heaps of plate are rang'd,
To be with each splenetic fashion changed.'

The Prospect of Plenty is another poem wherein Ramsay allows his reasoning powers to run away with him. As Chalmers remarks: 'To the chimerical hopes of inexhaustible riches from the project of the South Sea bubble, the poet now opposes the certain prospect of national wealth from the prosecution of the fisheries in the North Sea—thus judiciously pointing the attention of his countrymen to the solid fruits of patient industry, and contrasting these with the airy projects of idle speculation.' The poem points out that of industry the certain consequence is plenty, a gradual enlargement of all the comforts of society, the advancement of the useful, and the encouragement of the elegant arts, the cultivation of talents, the refinement of manners, the increase of population—all that contributes either to national prosperity or to the rational enjoyments of life. The composition and structure of the poem are less deserving of encomium than the wisdom of its precepts. Like *Content*, it is tedious and dull, yet there is one vigorous passage in it, beginning: 'A slothful pride! a kingdom's greatest curse,' and dealing with the evils arising from the separation of the classes, which has often been quoted. Nor must we forget *The Vision*, which in the opinion of many must rank amongst the best of Ramsay's productions. Published originally in the *Evergreen*, over the initials 'A. R. Scot,' for some time it was believed to be the work of a Scots poet, Alexander

Scott, who lived in the reign of Queen Mary. But Janet Ramsay put the matter beyond a doubt before her death by declaring the poem to have been written by her father. The merits of *The Vision* are considerable. The language is majestic and dignified, the ideas lofty, and the characters drawn with vigour and precision. Had the spelling not been so archaic, the poem would have been much more popular than it is.

For Horace, Ramsay always professed a deep admiration. Upon the style of the great Roman satirist he sought to model his 'Epistles,' which undoubtedly deserve something more than mere passing mention. In them Ramsay endeavours to give the friend, whom at the moment he addresses, a glimpse into the pursuits with which, for the time being, he was occupying himself. Taking this for his text, he digresses into apt and amusing dissertations on any subject of public, municipal, or social interest that might be engrossing the attention of the town. His epistles to Hamilton of Gilbertfield, to James Arbuckle, to the Earl of Dalhousie, to Mr. Aikman, to Sir W. Bennet, to William Starrat, to Joseph Burchet, to Somerville the poet, to Gay, to Clerk of Penicuik, and others, are altogether delightful—happy, cheery, humorous, gossipy productions, neither too full of fun to be frivolous, nor too didactic to be tiresome. Take, for example, his epistle to Robert Yarde of Devonshire,—how apt are his allusions, how racy his tit-bits of local news! He addresses the epistle

> ' Frae northern mountains clad with snaw,
> Where whistling winds incessant blaw,
> In time now when the curling-stane,
> Slides murm'ring o'er the icy plain ';

and he asks his correspondent how, under these conditions,

> ' What sprightly tale in verse can Yarde
> Expect frae a cauld Scottish bard,
> With brose and bannocks poorly fed,
> In hodden gray right hashly clad,
> Skelping o'er frozen hags with pingle,
> Picking up peats to beet his ingle,
> While sleet that freezes as it fa's,
> Theeks as with glass the divot wa's
> Of a laigh hut, where sax thegither
> Lie heads and thraws on craps of heather ? '

—this being a humorous allusion to the prevalent idea in England at the time, that the Scots were only a little better off than the savages of the South Seas.

Finally, in his translations, or rather paraphrases, from Horace, Ramsay was exceedingly happy. He made no pretensions to accuracy in his rendering of the precise words of the text. While preserving an approximation to the ideas of his original, he changes the local atmosphere and scene, and applies Horace's lines to the district around Edinburgh, wherewith he was so familiar. With rare skill this is achieved ; and while any lover of Horace can easily follow the ideas of the original, the non-classical reader is brought face to face with associations drawn from his own land as illustrative, by comparison and contrast, of the text of the great Roman. Few could have executed the task with greater truth ; fewer still with more felicity. Already I have cited a portion of Ramsay's rendering of Horace's famous Ode, *Vides ut alta stet nive candidum Soracte.* There are two other stanzas well worthy of quotation. Ramsay's rendering of the famous *Carpe diem*, etc., passage is all I have space for—

> ' Let neist day come as it thinks fit,
> The present minute's only ours;
> On pleasure let's employ our wit,
> And laugh at fortune's feckless powers.'

Reference has also been made to his apt translation of the ideas contained in Horace's 1st Ode to Maecenas, by making them express his own feelings towards Lord Dalhousie. Two of his aptest renderings of the original, however, were those of Horace's 18th Ode to Quintilius Varus (*Nullam, Vare, sacra vite prius severis arborem*), which our poet renders—

> 'O Binny, cou'd thae fields o' thine
> Bear, as in Gaul, the juicy vine,
> How sweet the bonny grape wad shine
>   On wa's where now
> Your apricock and peaches fine
>   Their branches bow.
>
> Since human life is but a blink,
> Then why should we its short joys sink :
> He disna live that canna link
>   The glass about ;
> Whan warm'd wi' wine, like men we think,
>   An' grow mair stout.'

The 31st Ode (B. 1.) to Apollo is thus felicitously rendered—

> ' Frae great Apollo, poets say,
> What would'st thou wish, what wadst thou hae
>   Whan thou bows at his shrine?
> Not Carse o' Gowrie's fertile field,
> Nor a' the flocks the Grampians yield
>   That are baith sleek and fine ;

> Not costly things, brocht frae afar,
>   As iv'ry, pearl and gems ;
> Nor those fair straths that watered are
>   Wi' Tay an' Tweed's smooth streams.
>   Which gentily and daintily
>   Eat down the flow'ry braes,
>   As greatly and quietly
>   They wimple to the seas.'

Ramsay had the misfortune never to have studied the
technique of his art, so that in no respect is he a master
of rhythm.   The majority of his longer poems, including
The Gentle Shepherd, are written in the ordinary heroic
measure,   so   popular   last   century   because   so   easily
manipulated.   His songs for the most part are written in
familiar metres, not calculated to puzzle any bonny
singing Bess as she danced and lilted on the village
green.   As a metrist, therefore, Ramsay can claim little
or no attention.   His poetry was the spontaneous ebulli-
tion of his own feelings, and for their expression he seized
upon the first measure that came to hand.

Such, then, is Ramsay !   In his matchless pastoral he
will ever live in the hearts of Scotsmen ; and were proof
needed, it would be found in the increasing numbers of
pilgrims who year by year journey to Carlops to visit the
scenes amongst which Peggy lived and loved.   To any
one save the historian and the antiquarian, the remainder
of his poetry may now be of little value,—probably of
none,—amidst the multifarious publications which day
by day issue from the press.   But by Scotsmen the
memory of the gentle, genial, lovable Allan will ever be
prized as that of one who, at a critical time, did more
to prevent Scottish national poetry from being wholly
absorbed by the mightier stream of English song than

any other man save Scott.   Worthy of such veneration,
then, is he, both as a poet and as a man; and though the
extravagant admiration wherewith he was regarded in his
own day, has given place to a soberer estimate of his
rank in the hierarchy of letters, yet Allan Ramsay can
never be held as other than one of the most delightful, if
he can no longer be rated as one of the greatest, of Scottish
poets.   That his immortal pastoral can ever be consigned
to the limbo of oblivion is as improbable as that our
posterity will forget *Tam o' Shanter* and the *Cotter's
Saturday Night.*   The opinion of Robert Burns regarding the permanence of his 'poetical forebear's' fame will
be cordially endorsed by every leal-hearted Scot, in whose
memory the sturdy manliness of Patie and the winning
beauty of Peggy are everlastingly enshrined—

> 'Yes! there is ane: a Scottish callan,
> There's ane; come forrit, honest Allan,
> Thou needna jouk behint the hallan,
>   A chiel' sae clever:
> The teeth o' time may gnaw Tantallan,
>   But thou's for ever!'

THE END.